# 訓練聽力　增加字彙

　　英語聽力是學習英語的重要一環，必須提早開始，長期訓練。而且要有計畫的反覆練習，絕不能只學聽單字認圖片，一定要聽句子，而且要逐漸拉長句子的內容，才能學習到英語的真諦。

　　本書是針對七、八、九年級學生的程度，循序漸進，逐步加強，期望能在 12 年國教的會考及特色招生考試中，一舉拿下聽力的滿分。本書的另一特色為在快樂學習中增加單字的記憶和使用能力，透過反覆的聽力訓練，不但大量增加字彙的累積，在不知不覺中也學會了說與寫的能力，可謂一舉數得，而且輕鬆易得。

　　為減輕學生的聽力障礙，本書將考題敘述的每個句子及答案，都精心譯為中文，以供學生參考。

　　在英語聽力測驗的出題「考點」中，我們歸納出下列幾個重點，請同學特別注意：

## 1. 隨時注意 7 個 W：who, when, what, where, which, why, how
　　也就是人、時、事、地、物、原因、狀態

## 2. 能夠與不能 (ability and inability)
　　常用字詞有：can, be able to, could, can't, couldn't, not be able to, neither

1)　　A: How many languages can you speak?
　　　B: I can/am able to speak three languages fluently.
　　翻譯：A：你能說幾種語言？
　　　　　B：我能流利的說三種語言。

2)　　A: Has he bought a new house?
　　　B: No. He's never been able to save money.
　　翻譯：A：他買新房子了嗎？
　　　　　B：不，他永遠沒有能力存錢。

3)　　A: I couldn't do the homework. It was too difficult.
　　　B: Neither could I.
　　翻譯：A：我不會做作業。太難了。
　　　　　B：我也不會。

## 3. 勸告與建議 (advice and suggestion)
　　常用字詞有：had better, I think, let's, OK, yes, good idea, sure, why not,

1)　　A: I've got a headache today.
　　　B: You'd better go to see the doctor./I think you should go to see the doctor.
　　翻譯：A：我今天頭痛。
　　　　　B：你最好去看醫生。我想你應該去看醫生。

2)　　A: I've got a terrible stomachache.

B: You'd better not go on working.

A: OK./All right./Thank you for your advice.

翻譯：A：我的胃痛死了。

　　　B：你最好不要上班。

　　　C：好的/沒問題/謝謝你的勸告。

3) A: Let's go, shall we?

B: Yes, let's./I'm afraid it's too early.

翻譯：A：我們走吧，要不要？

　　　B：好，走吧。/我怕太晚了。

4) A: What/How about going fishing now?

B: That's a good idea./That sounds interesting./Sure. Why not?

翻譯：A：現在去釣魚怎麼樣？

　　　B：好主意。/聽起來很有趣。/當然，有何不可？

5) A: Let's go to the concert.

B: I don't feel like it. Why don't we go to the beach instead?

翻譯：A：我們去聽音樂會吧。

　　　B：我不想去。我們為什麼不去海邊？

## 4. 同意與不同意 (agreement and disagreement)

常用字詞有：I think so. I hope so. I don't think so. I agree. I don't agree. So can I. Me too. Neither can I. I can't, either.

1) A: The book is interesting.

B: I think so, too.

翻譯：A：這本書很有趣。

　　　B：我也這麼想。

2) A: Do you think people will be able to live on the moon in the future?

B: I hope so, but I don't think so.

翻譯：A：你認為人類將來能住到月球上嗎？

　　　B：希望如此，但我不認為能夠。

3) A: This lesson is interesting, isn't it?

B: I don't think so./I'm afraid I can't agree with you./I'm afraid I don't quite agree with you./I'm afraid it isn't.

翻譯：A：這堂課很有趣，不是嗎？

　　　B：我不這樣認為。恐怕我無法同意你。我恐怕不十分同意你。恐怕不是這樣。

4) A: I can swim well.

B: So can I./Me too.

翻譯：A：我很會游泳。

　　　B：我也是。

5)　A: I can't play the guitar.

　　B: Neither can I./I can't, either.

　　翻譯：A：我不會彈吉他。

　　　　　B：我也不會。

## 5. 道歉（Apology）

常用字詞有：Sorry. I'm sorry about ....

A: Sorry./I'm terribly sorry about that.

B: That's all right./Never mind./Don't worry.

翻譯：A：抱歉。關於那件事我非常抱歉。

　　　B：沒關係。不要放在心上。不要擔心。

## 6. 讚賞（Appreciation）

常用字詞有：That's a good idea. That sounds interesting. Fantastic! Amazing! Well done ! That's wonderful.

1)　A: I've got the first prize.

　　B: Well done ! /You deserved to win./That's wonderful news.

　　翻譯：A：我得第一名。

　　　　　B：真棒。你實至名歸。真是個棒消息。

2)　A: We had a surprise birthday party on Saturday afternoon.

　　B: That was a super afternoon.

　　翻譯：A：星期六下午的生日聚會令人驚喜。

　　　　　B：那是個超棒的下午。

3)　A: He broke the world record for the two mile run.

　　B: Fantastic!/Amazing!

　　翻譯：A：他在兩英哩賽跑打破世界紀錄。

　　　　　B：了不起。又驚又喜。

## 7. 肯定與不肯定（certainty and uncertainty）

常用字詞有：sure, not sure, perhaps, maybe, possible, possibly,

1)　A: Are you sure?

　　B: Yes, I am./No, I'm not.

　　翻譯：A：你確定嗎？

B：是的，我確定。不，我不確定。

2) A: When will Mary go to school?
   B: Perhaps/Maybe she'll go at eight.
   翻譯：A：Mary 何時上學？
   　　　B：或許 8 歲。

3) A: His ambition is to be an architect.
   B: He'll possibly go to university after he leaves school.
   翻譯：A：他的願望是當建築師。
   　　　B：他離開學校後可能要念大學。

## 8. 比較 (Comparison)

常用字詞有：as...as..., not so... as..., more... than..., less...than...,

1) A: How tall is Sue?
   B: 1.6 meters. She's not so tall as Jane.
   A: What about Mary?
   B: She's as tall as Sue.
   翻譯：A：Sue 身高多少。
   　　　B：160 公分。她不像 Jane 那麼高。
   　　　A：那 Mary 呢？
   　　　B：她跟 Sue 一樣高。

2) A: Which is more important, electricity or water?
   B: It's hard to say.
   翻譯：A：哪個比較重要，水還是電？
   　　　B：很難說。

## 9. 關心 (Concern)

常用字詞有：Is anything wrong? What's the matter? What's wrong with ....?
What's the matter with ....? How's ......?

1) A: What's wrong with you?/What's the matter with you?
   B: I've got a cold.
   翻譯：A：你怎麼了？
   　　　B：我感冒了。

2) A: How's your mother?
   B: She's worse than yesterday.
   A: I'm sorry to hear that. Don't worry too much. She'll get better soon.
   翻譯：A：令堂狀況如何。
   　　　B：她比昨天更糟了。

> A：我聽了很遺憾。不用太擔心。她很快就會好一些。

4)　A: What's the matter?

B: I can't find my car key.

翻譯：A：發生甚麼事？

B：我找不到汽車鑰匙。

## 10. 詢問 (Inquiries)

常用字詞有：How, when, where, who, why, what

1)　A: Excuse me, how can I get to the railway station?

B: Take a No. 41 bus.

翻譯：A：對不起，要如何到火車站去？

B：搭 41 號公車。

2)　A: Excuse me. When does the next train leave for Kaohsuing?

B: 10 a.m.

翻譯：A：對不起。去高雄的下一班火車是甚麼時候？

B：上午十點。

3)　A: What's the weather like today?

B: It'll rain this afternoon.

翻譯：A：今天天氣如何？

B：下午會下雨。

4)　A: How far is your home from the school?

B: Five minutes by bike.

翻譯：A：你家距離學校有多遠？

B：騎單車 5 分鐘。

## 11. 意向 (Intentions)

常用字詞有：I'd like …, Would you like to…? What do you want …?

1)　A: What do you want to be in the future?

B: I want to be a businessman.

翻譯：A：你將來想當甚麼？

B：我想當生意人。

2)　A: Would you like to work at the South Pole in the future?

B: Yes, we'd love to.

翻譯：A：你將來喜歡在南極工作嗎？

B：是的，我會喜歡。

3)　A: I'd like fried eggs with peas and pork, too.

B: OK.

> 翻譯：A：我想要豆子、豬肉炒蛋。
>
> B：沒問題。

## 12. 喜歡、不喜歡/偏愛 (Likes, dislikes and preferences)

常用字詞有：like, dislike, prefer, enjoy

1) A: Which kind of apples do you prefer, red ones or green ones?

B: Green ones.

翻譯：A：你比較喜歡哪一種蘋果，紅的還是綠的？

B：綠的。

2) A: Do you enjoy music or dance?

B: I enjoy music.

翻譯：A：你喜歡音樂還是跳舞？

B：我喜歡音樂。

3) A: How did you like the play?

B: It was wonderful.

翻譯：A：這齣戲你覺得如何？

B：很棒。

## 13. 提供 (Offers)

常用字詞有：Can I ....? Let me .... What can I ...? Would you like ...?

1) A: Can I help you?

B: Yes, please.

翻譯：A：可以幫你忙嗎？

B：是的，謝謝。

2) A: Let me help you.

B: Thanks.

翻譯：A：我來幫你忙。

B：謝謝。

3) A: Would you like a drink?

B: That's very kind of you.

翻譯：A：要來杯飲料嗎？

B：你真好意。

4) A: Shall I get a trolley for you?

B: No, thanks.

翻譯：A：要我拿輛手推車給你嗎？

B：不用，謝謝。

十二年國教特色招生及會考

# 全新英語聽力測驗

〔會考總複習〕

## 目　次

# 夏朵英文

## 全新英語聽力會考總複習試題

# Unit 1

---

I、Listen and choose the right picture.（根據你所聽到的內容,選出相應的圖片。）（6分）

A                B                C

D          E          F          G

1. _____     2. _____     3. _____

4. _____     5. _____     6. _____

---

II、Listen to the dialogue and choose the best answer to the question. （根據你所聽到的對話和問題，選出最恰當的答案。）（10分）

( ) 7.   (A)Alice's cousin.        (B)Alice's brother.
       (C)Alice's sister.          (D)Alice's pen-friend.

( ) 8.   (A)German.              (B)Japanese.
       (C)Korean.               (D)Chinese.

( ) 9.   (A)In a bookstore.       (B)In a library.
       (C)In a hospital.         (D)In a cinema.

( ) 10. (A)When we need to make friends. (B)Why we need to make friends.
       (C)When to make friends.      (D)How to make friends.

( ) 11. (A)Monday.            (B)Sunday.
       (C)Tuesday.          (D)Wednesday.

( ) 12. (A)By visiting their houses. (B)By writing ordinary mails.
　　　　(C)By writing e-mails. (D)By phone.

( ) 13. (A)By underground. (B)By taxi.
　　　　(C)By bus. (D)On foot.

( ) 14. (A)Cartoons. (B)Action movies.
　　　　(C)Horror movies. (D)Adventure movies.

( ) 15. (A)It's impossible to make real friends with so many people.
　　　　(B)In fact, the woman has no friends around her.
　　　　(C)The woman is telling a lie and she is dishonest.
　　　　(D)The man wants to tell the woman not to make many friends.

( ) 16. (A)At 8. (B)At 7:45.
　　　　(C)At 7:55. (D)At 8:05.

---

**Ⅲ、Listen to the passage and tell whether the following statements are true or false.**
（判斷下列句子是否符合你听到的短文内容,符合用 T 表示,不符合用 F 表示）（7分）

( ) 17. Human beings can't do without friends.

( ) 18. The writer doesn't want her friends to come to her when she is very sad.

( ) 19. According to the writer, a real friend is the same as a precious pearl.

( ) 20. To have the same hobbies or interests is the first thing that people consider when they make friends.

( ) 21. The writer wants to make friends with those who have enough power.

( ) 22. The writer doesn't want to make friends with people who wear glasses.

( ) 23. The support the writer gives to her friend will never change all her life.

---

**Ⅳ、Listen to the passage and fill in the blanks with proper words.**（聽短文,用最恰當的填空,每格限填一詞）（共7分）

- The nationality of the pen-friend is __24__.
- Now he studies in Grade __25__ in a Junior High School.
- The subjects he does well in are __26__ and math.
- The pen-friend __27__ me to teach him Chinese at the beginning.
- He seems to have lots of __28__.
- In his letters, he shares with me many __29__ in his country.
- I hope to meet him in China so that we can __30__ with each other better.

24. _____　　25. _____　　26. _____　　27. _____

28. _____　　29. _____　　30. _____

# 夏朵英文
## 全新英語聽力會考總複習試題
# Unit 2

Ⅰ、Listen and choose the right picture.（根據你所聽到的內容,選出相應的圖片。）（6 分）

A    B    C

D    E    F    G

1. _____   2. _____   3. _____

4. _____   5. _____   6. _____

Ⅱ、Listen to the dialogue and choose the best answer to the question. （根據你所聽到的對話和問題，選出最恰當的答案。）（10 分）

( ) 7. (A)A policeman.    (B)A nurse.

(C)A secretary.    (D)A doctor.

( ) 8. (A)At 9 o'clock.    (B)At 8:30.

(C)At 8:20.    (D)At 7:50.

( ) 9. (A)In a library.    (B)In a post office.

(C)In a bookstore.    (D)At the airport.

( ) 10. (A)The guitar.    (B)The piano.

(C)The violin.    (D)The drum.

( ) 11. (A)Buying some new clothes will make babies smile.

(B)Dressing babies the clothes they like will make them smile.

(C)Showing lovely dolls will make babies smile.

(D)Dressing babies up like dolls will make them smile.

( ) 12. (A)The girl doesn't know her teachers.
(B)The boy thinks nobody is busy.
(C)The girl isn't hard working.
(D)The boy doesn't agree with the girl.

( ) 13. (A)Eating much spicy food
(B)Not taking medicine.
(C)Not eating breakfast regularly.
(D)Enjoy too many fruits.

( ) 14. (A)Lucy works harder than her husband.
(B)Her husband works very hard.
(C)Her husband likes drinking.
(D)She works harder than her husband.

( ) 15. (A)Shanghai.　　　　　　　(B)China.
(C)Canada.　　　　　　　(D)Britain.

( ) 16. (A)Mike's mother.　　　　　(B)Mike's teacher.
(C)Mike's sister.　　　　　(D)Mike's classmate.

---

**Ⅲ、Listen to the passage and tell whether the following statements are true or false.**
（判斷下列句子是否符合你听到的短文内容,符合用 T 表示,不符合用 F 表示）（7分）

---

( ) 17. The group of monkeys lived an exciting and rich life in a forest.

( ) 18. Monkey David stole a watch from a traveler.

( ) 19. No monkeys knew how to use the watch and they threw it away.

( ) 20. The watch helped David to be the king of the group.

( ) 21. David could tell more accurate time with the help of more watches.

( ) 22. Other monkeys were always satisfied with David's job.

( ) 23. From the story, we can conclude that watches are not as helpful as the sun.

---

**Ⅳ、Listen to the passage and fill in the blanks with proper words.**（聽短文,用最恰當的填空,每格限填一詞）（共7分）

---

- We need money for __24__ and food and to pay for houses.
- Work can help us feel that we are __25__ as well.
- It's hard for a new __26__ to find a good job immediately.
- When you work, you can gather a lot of __27__ for future jobs.
- __28__ study is a trend to make sure that we can keep ourselves up with the high developing society.

- We have no __29__ but to adjust our thoughts to be ready to learn anything at any time.
- Susan has a right attitude (態度) towards __30__.

24. _____ 25. _____ 26. _____ 27. _____
28. _____ 29. _____ 30. _____

# 夏朵英文
## 全新英語聽力會考總複習試題
# Unit 3

I、Listen and choose the right picture.（根據你所聽到的內容,選出相應的圖片。）（6分）

A　　　　　　　　B　　　　　　　　C

D　　　　　　　　E　　　　　　　　F　　　　　　　　G

1. ＿＿＿＿＿＿　2. ＿＿＿＿＿＿　3. ＿＿＿＿＿＿
4. ＿＿＿＿＿＿　5. ＿＿＿＿＿＿　6. ＿＿＿＿＿＿

II、Listen to the dialogue and choose the best answer to the question. （根據你所聽到的對話和問題，選出最恰當的答案。）（10分）

（　）7.　(A)They met with the same problem in the last Unit.
　　　　(B)The boy can find the solution on the last page of a book.
　　　　(C)The boy wanted the girl to do more revision.
　　　　(D)The girl didn't know the solution at all.

（　）8.　(A)She became too fat.　　　　(B)She fell off her bike.
　　　　(C)Her leg was injured.　　　　(D)A boy knocked her down.

（　）9.　(A)Red.　　　　　　　　　　(B)White.
　　　　(C)Blue.　　　　　　　　　　(D)Black.

（　）10.　(A)He didn't eat up his dinner.
　　　　(B)He played computer games for too long.
　　　　(C)He was sick.
　　　　(D)He didn't wash his dish.

( ) 11. (A)Which museum to visit.
(B)How to get tickets.
(C)Where the entrance to the museum is.
(D)When to see the museum.

( ) 12. (A)The man should not buy the apartment.
(B)The man should save money in the bank.
(C)The man should sell all his belongings.
(D)The man should borrow money from the bank.

( ) 13. (A)Once. (B)Twice.
(C)Three times. (D)Never.

( ) 14. (A)In the library. (B)In the classroom.
(C)In the art room. (D)At home.

( ) 15. (A)Fine. (B)Cloudy.
(C)Rainy. (D)Foggy.

( ) 16. (A)It has a new system. (B)It has high speed.
(C)It's fashionable. (D)It's cheap.

---

Ⅲ、Listen to the passage and tell whether the following statements are true or false.
（判斷下列句子是否符合你听到的短文内容,符合用 T 表示,不符合用 F 表示）(7 分)

( ) 17. Joe Cole is a basketball player and he is talented.

( ) 18. Joe Cole performed wonderfully at the 2010 World Cup.

( ) 19. Cole's coach doesn't think it wise for Cole to change a team.

( ) 20. Steve and Cole played in one team for nearly 3 years.

( ) 21. Steve thinks the reason why Cole isn't successful is that he doesn't work hard.

( ) 22. The old team didn't give Joe Cole the right role.

( ) 23. If a person has ability, he or she will always succeed.

---

Ⅳ、Listen to the passage and fill in the blanks with proper words.（聽短文,用最恰當的填空,每格限填一詞）（共 7 分）

- The man feels very glad to stand here and give people a short __24__.

- The man thinks some takers take others' hard work for granted instead of running after something __25__.

- Because of several reasons, more and more takers are __26__ in our society.

- A giver should __27__ taking with giving.

- A giver should help the others who are in __28__.

- To be a giver doesn't mean that you shouldn't ask for material __29__.
- We can get __30__ from living in the way of learning to be a good giver.

24. _____    25. _____    26. _____    27. _____

28. _____    29. _____    30. _____

# 夏朵英文

## 全新英語聽力會考總複習試題
## Unit 4

Ⅰ、Listen and choose the right picture.（根據你所聽到的內容,選出相應的圖片。）（6分）

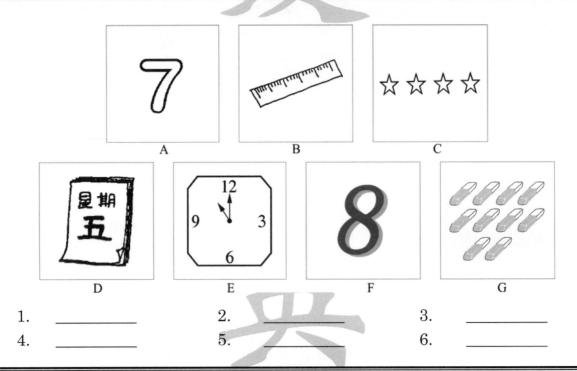

1. ＿＿＿＿＿　　2. ＿＿＿＿＿　　3. ＿＿＿＿＿

4. ＿＿＿＿＿　　5. ＿＿＿＿＿　　6. ＿＿＿＿＿

Ⅱ、Listen to the dialogue and choose the best answer to the question. （根據你所聽到的對話和問題，選出最恰當的答案。）（10分）

( ) 7. (A)16. (B)40. (C)22. (D)18.

( ) 8. (A)7:50. (B)10:50. (C)9:30. (D)11:50.

( ) 9. (A)For 13 days. (B)For 2 weeks. (C)For 6 days. (D)For 7 days.

( ) 10. (A)8. (B)6. (C)3. (D)7.

( ) 11. (A)10 yuan. (B)99 yuan. (C)90 yuan. (D)100 yuan.

( ) 12. (A)25 min. (B)35 min. (C)15 min. (D)20 min.

( ) 13. (A)61213009. (B)62131009. (C)62131008. (D)61213008.

( ) 14. (A)1 liter. (B)2 liters. (C)0.5 liter. (D)0.25 liter.

( ) 15. (A)4. (B)5. (C)3. (D)6.

( ) 16. (A)March 1st. (B)Feb. 29rd. (C)Feb. 28th. (D)Feb. 27th.

Ⅲ、Listen to the passage and tell whether the following statements are true or false.（判斷下列句子是否符合你听到的短文內容,符合用 T 表示,不符合用 F 表示）（7分）

（　）17. In the writer's opinion, one is an unlucky number.

（　）18. The earthquake that happened in Taiwan in 2001 killed about 2,000 people.

（　）19. The terrorists attacked the U.S. on 9·11 because they thought one was really a bad number.

（　）20. The airplanes crashed into the tall buildings and luckily flew back to the air base.

（　）21. On 7·11, a big typhoon attacked Taiwan in 2001.

（　）22. Some people died in the typhoon because the wind took them away.

（　）23. According to the writer, January has the most days on which he will be quite careful.

Ⅳ、Listen to the passage and fill in the blanks with proper words.（聽短文,用最恰當的填空,每格限填一詞）（共7分）

- A serious earthquake hit New Zealand at around __24__ a.m. local time.

- Christchurch, New Zealand's second-largest city has a population of about __25__ people.

- The U.S. Geological Survey at first reported it at 7.4 but later changed its figure to __26__.

- The quake lasted up to __27__ seconds.

- About __28__ earthquakes happen in New Zealand every year.

- The last serious earthquake in New Zealand took place in __29__.

- __30__ people lost their lives in the last serious earthquake.

24. _____  25. _____  26. _____  27. _____

28. _____  29. _____  30. _____

# 夏朵英文

## 全新英語聽力會考總複習試題

# Unit 5

---

I、Listen and choose the right picture.（根據你聽到的內容,選出相應的圖片。）（6分）

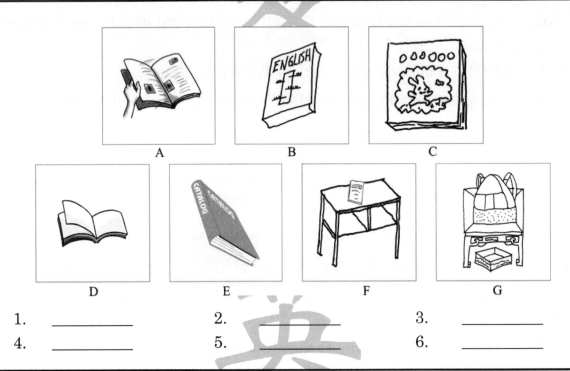

A　　　　　　　　B　　　　　　　　C

D　　　　　　　E　　　　　　　F　　　　　　　G

1. _____　　2. _____　　3. _____

4. _____　　5. _____　　6. _____

---

II、Listen to the dialogue and choose the best answer to the question.　（根據你所聽到的對話和問題，選出最恰當的答案。）（10分）

(　　) 7.　(A)78 pages.　　　　　　　　(B)80 pages.
　　　　　(C)160 pages.　　　　　　　(D)156 pages.

(　　) 8.　(A)The girl.　　　　　　　　(B)The boy.
　　　　　(C)The boy's mother.　　　　(D)The girl's mother.

(　　) 9.　(A)This is the best book she has ever read.
　　　　　(B)She doesn't like the book at all.
　　　　　(C)She thinks there is a book better than this.
　　　　　(D)She doesn't think it is the best book.

(　　) 10.　(A)From the library.　　　　(B)From the bookstore.
　　　　　(C)From his parents.　　　　(D)From the girl.

(   ) 11. (A)The girl doesn't enjoy the book.
     (B)The girl thinks it is an attractive book.
     (C)The girl doesn't know how to answer the question.
     (D)The girl suggests we read the book.

(   ) 12. (A)On the sofa.                              (B)On the table.
     (C)Under the table.                           (D)In his
     schoolbag.

(   ) 13. (A)120 yuan.                                (B)150 yuan.
     (C)156 yuan.                                  (D)136 yuan.

(   ) 14. Because books are easy to understand.
     (B)Because films don't describe details as well as books.
     (C)Because films are less interesting than books.
     (D)Because books are the man's favorite.

(   ) 15. (A)Martin.                                  (B)Mike.
     (C)May.                                       (D)Mary.

(   ) 16. (A)She suggests the boy read the book.
     (B)She agrees with the boy.
     (C)She doesn't like the cover of the book.
     (D)She won't buy the book.

---

Ⅲ、Listen to the passage and tell whether the following statements are true or false.
（判斷下列句子是否符合你听到的短文内容,符合用 T 表示,不符合用 F 表示）（7分）

(   ) 17. To be a babysitter is the writer's first job.

(   ) 18. Cindy is the name of one of the babies the writer is going to take care of.

(   ) 19. When the writer's mom was talking with her friend last week, the writer was sitting in her bedroom.

(   ) 20. When the writer was waving her arms to her mom, her mom understood what the writer meant.

(   ) 21. Mrs. Barb was a little bit worried about the writer, but the writer never gave up.

(   ) 22. The writer is going to do the job four times a week.

(   ) 23. The writer has little confidence in getting on well with the babies.

---

Ⅳ、Listen to the passage and fill in the blanks with proper words.（聽短文,用最恰當的填空,每格限填一詞）（共7分）

- Please __24__ the five steps if you want to have a great lunch.
- One: Choose fruits and vegetables which can make your __25__ colorful.

- Two: Know the facts about fat. Eat less often and in __26__ portions.
- Three: Drinks are also good __27__.
- Four: Balance your lunch and a __28__ order of hot dogs isn't a balanced one.
- Five: __29__ the lunch up. Eat different kinds of food.
- Different foods provide a __30__ of nutrients.

24. _____    25. _____    26. _____    27. _____

28. _____    29. _____    30. _____

# 夏朵英文

## 全新英語聽力會考總複習試題

# Unit 6

---

I、Listen and choose the right picture.（根據你所聽到的內容,選出相應的圖片。）（6 分）

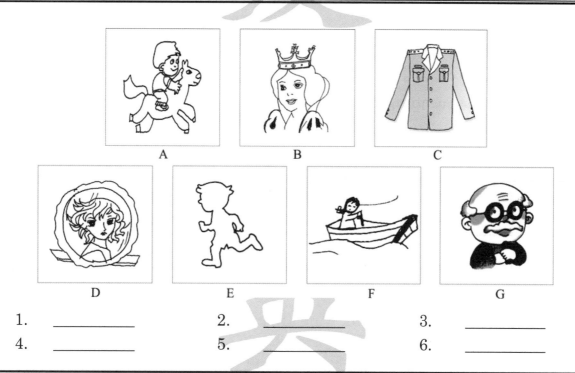

A      B      C

D      E      F      G

1. _____      2. _____      3. _____

4. _____      5. _____      6. _____

---

II、Listen to the dialogue and choose the best answer to the question. （根據你所聽到的對話和問題，選出最恰當的答案。）（10 分）

(　) 7.   (A)He isn't interested in the science fiction.
       (B)He is much interested in the science fiction.
       (C)He has a little interest in the science fiction.
       (D)He likes the book.

(　) 8.   (A)She wrote a book.      (B)She phoned Danny.
       (C)She talked with Danny.      (D)She read a book.

(　) 9.   (A)50.      (B)14.
       (C)16.      (D)51.

(　) 10.   (A)He has to have piano lessons outside.
       (B)He has to take care of her mother.
       (C)He has no pocket money.
       (D)He has to listen to his mother.

( ) 11. (A)To buy books. (B)To pick up rubbish.
(C)To play in Zhongshan Park. (D)To visit Jason.

( ) 12. (A)10:30. (B)11:10.
(C)10:50. (D)11:35.

( ) 13. (A)He will meet Roy at school.
(B)He will take care of the sick grandmother.
(C)He will go to Beijing for business.
(D)He will attend the parent meeting.

( ) 14. (A)At ten o'clock. (B)At ten thirty.
(C)At eleven o'clock. (D)At eleven thirty.

( ) 15. (A)Black tea. (B)Black coffee.
(C)Milk tea. (D)Coffee with milk.

( ) 16. (A)Guess meanings. (B)Use
dictionaries.
(C)Take notes. (D)Record problems.

---

Ⅲ、Listen to the passage and tell whether the following statements are true or false.
（判斷下列句子是否符合你听到的短文內容,符合用 T 表示,不符合用 F 表示）（7分）

( ) 17. Mr. Jackson's job was to move machines into his factory.

( ) 18. Mr. Jackson could earn more money because he was good at driving.

( ) 19. Mr. Jackson often drank wine after supper.

( ) 20. Mr. Jackson agreed to drink with his friend and drank a little.

( ) 21. Mr. Jackson didn't stop with the red light on and was caught by the police at the crossing.

( ) 22. When Mr. Jackson drank again, his wife got angry and argued with him seriously.

( ) 23. The next morning, when Mrs. Jackson told her husband that he drank much, Mr. Jackson didn't want to admit.

---

Ⅳ、Listen to the passage and fill in the blanks with proper words.（聽短文,用最恰當的填空,每格限填一詞）（共7分）

- The __24__ Sky Column in Zhangjiajie will now be known as the Avatar Mountain.

- The mountain had been used as the basis for Avatar's __25__ world of Pandora.

- Avatar has become the most __26__ film in China.

- A Hollywood photographer's __27__ helped create the world of Avatar.

- Zhangjiajie __28__ to attract more tourists by renaming the mountains.

- The government website has used the slogan "Pandora is __29__ but Zhangjiajie is near".

- The film Avatar has been showing on __30__ screens throughout China.

-

24. _____    25. _____    26. _____    27. _____

28. _____    29. _____    30. _____

# 夏朵英文

全新英語聽力會考總複習試題

# Unit 7

---

Ⅰ、Listen and choose the right picture.（根據你所聽到的內容,選出相應的圖片。）（6 分）

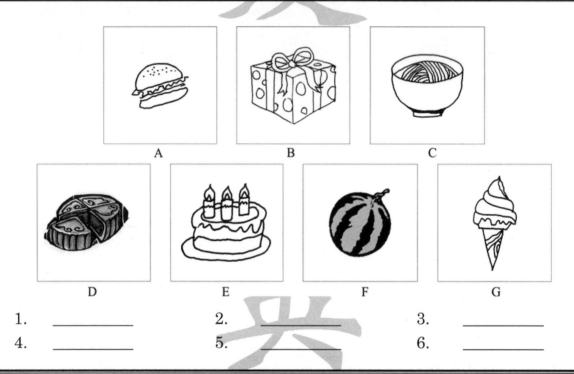

A       B       C

D       E       F       G

1. _____     2. _____     3. _____

4. _____     5. _____     6. _____

---

Ⅱ、Listen to the dialogue and choose the best answer to the question. （根據你所聽到的對話和問題，選出最恰當的答案。）（10 分）

( ) 7.　(A)Milk.　　　(B)Eggs.　　　(C)Bacon.　　　(D)Bread.

( ) 8.　(A)Nov. 2nd.　(B)Oct. 31st.　(C)Nov. 3rd.　(D)Nov. 4th.

( ) 9.　(A)His workmate.　　　　(B)His classmate.
　　　　(C)His deskmate.　　　　(D)His roommate.

( ) 10.　(A)At the cinema.　　　　(B)In the hospital.
　　　　(C)At a library.　　　　(D)At school.

( ) 11.　(A)At 4 o'clock.　(B)At 3:30.　(C)At 3 o'clock.　(D)At 2:30.

( ) 12.　(A)Exciting.　(B)Meaningful.　(C)Terrible.　(D)Interesting.

( ) 13.　(A)A doctor.　(B)A policeman.　(C)A teacher.　(D)A worker.

( ) 14.　(A)He smoked a lot.　　　　(B)He began to smoke.
　　　　(C)He had a sore throat.　　(D)He threw the cigarettes away.

（　）15.　(A)In a restaurant.　　　　　　　(B)At school.

（C)In the kitchen.　　　　　　　(D)In a flower market.

（　）16.　(A)She is too old and she wants to give up learning more.

(B)She thinks it is wise to learn at one's early age.

(C)She won't stop learning till her death.

(D)She is afraid of learning too much as it wastes time.

---

**Ⅲ、Listen to the passage and tell whether the following statements are true or false.**

（判斷下列句子是否符合你听到的短文内容,符合用 T 表示,不符合用 F 表示）（7分）

（　）17.　Jim lived alone in another town as he worked there.

（　）18.　Jim didn't like housework and he always made his flat dusty and untidy.

（　）19.　Mrs. Roper was introduced to Jim and came to see Jim the next morning.

（　）20.　Jim left a message on a paper to tell Mrs. Roper to clean the mirror.

（　）21.　Jim was always coughing badly whenever he breathed.

（　）22.　The cough medicine Mrs. Roper prepared would make Jim deeply moved.

（　）23.　Mrs. Roper misunderstood Jim's message.

---

**Ⅳ、Listen to the passage and fill in the blanks with proper words.**（聽短文,用最恰當的填空,每格限填一词）（共 7 分）

● Healthy skin is __24__ to all kinds of people.

● Keeping your hands clean can stop germs from being __25__ to other places.

● We'd better use warm water and mild __26__ to wash hands.

● Remember to clean the __27__ under your arms or behind your ears during a bath.

● It is wise to wash your face once or twice __28__ with warm water.

● Drinking enough water makes your skin brighter and __29__.

● You will have fewer __30__ problems if you take good care of your skin.

24. _____　　25. _____　　26. _____　　27. _____

28. _____　　29. _____　　30. _____

# 夏朵英文

## 全新英語聽力會考總複習試題

# Unit 8

---

Ⅰ、Listen and choose the right picture.（根據你所聽到的內容,選出相應的圖片。）（6分）

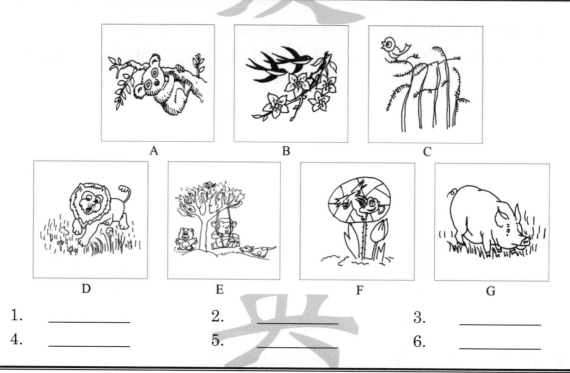

1. _____    2. _____    3. _____

4. _____    5. _____    6. _____

---

Ⅱ、Listen to the dialogue and choose the best answer to the question. （根據你所聽到的對話和問題，選出最恰當的答案。）（10分）

(　　) 7.　(A)Have a picnic.　　　　　　(B)Plant trees.
　　　　　(C)Go boating.　　　　　　　(D)Play for fun.

(　　) 8.　(A)25.　　　　　　　　　　　(B)40.
　　　　　(C)70.　　　　　　　　　　　(D)50.

(　　) 9.　(A)On Thursday.　　　　　　(B)On Saturday.
　　　　　(C)On Friday.　　　　　　　(D)On Monday.

(　　) 10.　(A)Physics.　　　　　　　　(B)Math.
　　　　　(C)Chinese.　　　　　　　　(D)English.

(　　) 11.　(A)There isn't enough sunshine.　(B)The kitchen is small.
　　　　　(C)Life there is inconvenient.　(D)The price of the flat is very high.

(　　) 12.　(A)13671789110.　　　　　　(B)13617789910.
　　　　　(C)13617789110.　　　　　　(D)13617889910.

( ) 13. (A)A doctor. (B)A teacher. (C)A nurse. (D)A boss.

( ) 14. (A)To a restaurant. (B)To a dairy.
(C)To a fridge. (D)To a supermarket.

( ) 15. (A)50 min. (B)60 min.
(C)10 min. (D)70 min.

( ) 16. (A)Because there are many advertisements.
(B)Because TV has taken the place of newspapers.
(C)Because he can hardly see clearly the letters in newspapers.
(D)Because he likes moving pictures.

---

**Ⅲ、Listen to the passage and tell whether the following statements are true or false.**
（判斷下列句子是否符合你听到的短文内容,符合用 T 表示,不符合用 F 表示）（7 分）

( ) 17. In the past, most people walked to factories quite early.

( ) 18. Only the Internet helps people to work from home.

( ) 19. When neighbors are leaving for their factories, you may be having a bath.

( ) 20. Video telephones make it possible talking with more people at the same time.

( ) 21. The pay for the video telephones depends on the number of participants.

( ) 22. You don't need to stop your work if you are not hungry at noon.

( ) 23. Working from home helps save a lot of time that can be spent working and even relaxing.

---

**Ⅳ、Listen to the passage and fill in the blanks with proper words.** （聽短文,用最恰當的填空,每格限填一詞）（共 7 分）

● Earth Hour started in a country named __24__.

● In 2008, even the Golden Gate __25__ stood in darkness.

● In 2009, __26__ countries took part in Earth Hour.

● In 2010, Earth Hour was on . The date was March __27__.

● Earth Hour 2010 is a call for all human beings to stand up and take __28__.

● All famous buildings from __29__ to Asia and the Americas stood in darkness.

● We hold Earth Hour just to celebrate the only thing we have in __30__—our planet.

24. _____    25. _____    26. _____    27. _____

28. _____    29. _____    30. _____

# 夏朵英文

## 全新英語聽力會考總複習試題

## Unit 9

I、Listen and choose the right picture.（根據你所聽到的內容,選出相應的圖片。）（6分）

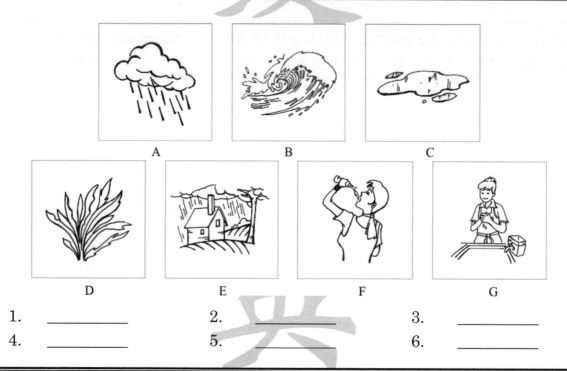

A    B    C

D    E    F    G

1. _____  2. _____  3. _____

4. _____  5. _____  6. _____

II、Listen to the dialogue and choose the best answer to the question. （根據你所聽到的對話和問題，選出最恰當的答案。）（10分）

(  ) 7.  (A)Water.   (B)Coffee.   (C)Tea.   (D)Wine.

(  ) 8.  (A)18 dollars.  (B)80 dollars.  (C)480 dollars.  (D)108 dollars.

(  ) 9.  (A)Turn off the tap.     (B)Use less water.

    (C)Educate those who waste water.  (D)Tell others to drink less.

(  ) 10.  (A)Seeing the doctor.    (B)Cooking.

    (C)Having dinner.     (D)Lying in bed.

(  ) 11.  (A)Basketball.     (B)Swimming.

    (C)Tennis.      (D)Football.

(  ) 12.  (A)She doesn't want to send an email.

    (B)She has been controlled by the computer.

    (C)Her parents asked her to write on the paper.

    (D)She is not allowed to use the computer.

( ) 13. (A)In the U.K. (B)In the U.S.A.
(C)In the P.R.C. (D)In the U.N.

( ) 14. (A)A movie. (B)A book. (C)A magazine. (D)A story.

( ) 15. (A)She ate much spicy food. (B)She liked eating too much.
(C)She didn't have her breakfast. (D)She was not feeling well.

( ) 16. (A)She wants the boy never to be late again.
(B)She isn't angry with the boy.
(C)She wants the boy never to come to the fair.
(D)She doesn't care about the boy.

---

**III、Listen to the passage and tell whether the following statements are true or false.**
（判斷下列句子是否符合你听到的短文內容,符合用 T 表示,不符合用 F 表示）（7分）

( ) 17. Yellowstone is the first park in America and even in the world.

( ) 18. Yellowstone has been open for more than 130 years.

( ) 19. There are no cages in Yellowstone, but animals are unable to live in a natural way.

( ) 20. Animals in Yellowstone are quite happy if people feed food to them.

( ) 21. Hunting animals in Yellowstone will bring damage to animals' life.

( ) 22. People and wild animals live together peacefully in Yellowstone.

( ) 23. In most zoos, animals are kept in cages.

---

**IV、Listen to the passage and fill in the blanks with proper words.** （聽短文,用最恰當的填空,每格限填一詞）（共7分）

● Rivers, as a kind of __24__ resources, are quite important.

● At least one river __25__ through a country and it plays an important role.

● The Nile is the longest river worldwide and is the lifeline of __26__.

● Large ships can go about thousands of miles upon the Amazon because it is so __27__ and wide.

● Rivers also give food, water to drink, water to irrigate __28__, and chances for fun.

● The problem of river pollution is __29__ by chemicals and other materials from large cities or industries located upon rivers.

● Keeping rivers clean can make human beings enjoy the __30__ of this natural resource.

24. _____    25. _____    26. _____    27. _____

28. _____    29. _____    30. _____

# 夏朵英文

# Unit 10

---

I、Listen and choose the right picture.（根據你所聽到的內容,選出相應的圖片。）（6分）

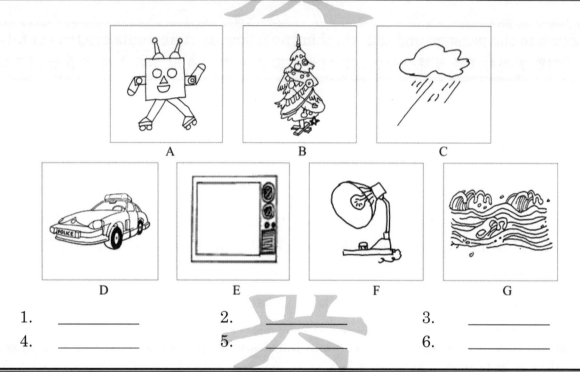

A　　　　　　　B　　　　　　　C

D　　　　　E　　　　　F　　　　　G

1. _____　　　2. _____　　　3. _____

4. _____　　　5. _____　　　6. _____

---

II、Listen to the dialogue and choose the best answer to the question. （根據你所聽到的對話和問題，選出最恰當的答案。）（10分）

(　)7.　(A)Turn on the fan.　　　　　　(B)Clean the fan.
　　　　(C)Turn off the fan.　　　　　(D)Carry the fan.

(　)8.　(A)The quality of the radio is poor.
　　　　(B)There is something wrong with some parts of the radio.
　　　　(C)The radio is broken.
　　　　(D)The batteries need changing.

(　)9.　(A)Five.　　　　　　　　　　(B)Six.
　　　　(C)Four.　　　　　　　　　　(D)Three.

(　)10.　(A)400 yuan.　　　　　　　　(B)460 yuan.
　　　　(C)230 yuan.　　　　　　　　(D)200 yuan.

(　)11.　(A)Seeing a film.　　　　　　　(B)Watching TV.
　　　　(C)Swimming across the channel.　(D)Discussing the latest film.

( ) 12. (A)Because of something wrong with the wire.
(B)Because all the lights are broken.
(C)Because of the bad weather.
(D)Because of a special program.

( ) 13. (A)40 minutes.      (B)20 minutes.
(C)Half an hour.      (D)10 minutes.

( ) 14. (A)He doesn't know how to do it.
(B)He should wash his hands first.
(C)His hands are wet.
(D)His mother loves him very much.

( ) 15. (A)Fire power.      (B)Solar energy.
(C)Water power.      (D)Wind power.

( ) 16. (A)About wave.      (B)About electricity.
(C)About heat.      (D)About light.

---

Ⅲ、Listen to the passage and tell whether the following statements are true or false.
（判斷下列句子是否符合你听到的短文内容,符合用 T 表示,不符合用 F 表示）（7分）

( ) 17. One day, Richard Brody received a letter and a piano from a company in New York.

( ) 18. Richard Brody was clever enough not to send the 10 dollars to the company.

( ) 19. The company really sent Richard Brody a piano that could make a sound.

( ) 20. The plastic piano cost 2 dollars more than the money Richard sent to the company.

( ) 21. Richard is just one of those who send money to dishonest companies every year.

( ) 22. About 500 dollars are sent to such companies every year by Americans.

( ) 23. Actually, Richard belongs to the lucky as 10 dollars is after all a small amount.

---

Ⅳ、Listen to the passage and fill in the blanks with proper words.（聽短文,用最恰當的填空,每格限填一詞）（共7分）

- Samuel Morse invented the __24__ around 1840.
- Thomas Edison invented lighting in __25__.
- In all, the way we live has been __26__ by electricity.

- The practical uses for electricity as well as the __27__ for its production grew.

- Some power __28__ are located more than 1,000miles from us.

- The __29__ sources of energy used to make electricity for business were coal-fired steam and water power.

- Electricity has become the most essential __30__ in our daily life.

24. _____    25. _____    26. _____    27. _____

28. _____    29. _____    30. _____

# 夏朵英文

全新英語聽力會考總複習試題

# Unit 11

---

I、Listen and choose the right picture.（根據你所聽到的內容,選出相應的圖片。）（6 分）

A       B       C

D       E       F       G

1. _____  2. _____  3. _____

4. _____  5. _____  6. _____

---

II、Listen to the dialogue and choose the best answer to the question. （根據你所聽到的對話和問題，選出最恰當的答案。）（10 分）

( ) 7. (A)Every day.         (B)Once a week.
       (C)Twice a month.      (D)Every month.

( ) 8. (A)Because his teacher wanted to borrow the newspapers.
       (B)Because reading newspapers is his favorite activity.
       (C)Because it is his homework.
       (D)Because he is looking for someone he wants to meet.

( ) 9. (A)At 3:30.          (B)At 4:00.
       (C)At 3:00.          (D)She didn't get the newspaper.

( ) 10. (A)At a drug store.      (B)In the boy's home.
       (C)In a reading room.     (D)In a dining room.

( ) 11. (A)Watching TV.       (B)Reading a newspaper.
       (C)Listening to the radio.   (D)Chatting on the Internet.

( ) 12. (A)Take some medicine. (B)Have a break.
(C)Speak more. (D)Go to the doctor's.

( ) 13. (A)The man agrees with the woman.
(B)The man thinks it is impossible for the woman to win.
(C)The man disagrees with the woman.
(D)The man thinks actions speak louder than words.

( ) 14. (A)In the pencil-box. (B)On the shelf.
(C)On the desk. (D)In a wooden box.

( ) 15. (A)A big balcony. (B)A study.
(C)Three bathrooms. (D)A small bathroom.

( ) 16. (A)She is good at English. (B)She likes writing diaries.
(C)She enjoys writing songs. (D)She sings English songs well.

---

Ⅲ、Listen to the passage and tell whether the following statements are true or false.
（判斷下列句子是否符合你听到的短文内容,符合用 T 表示,不符合用 F 表示）（7 分）

( ) 17. Bill studied in Grade Nine and had to go to school very early.

( ) 18. Newspapers are sent to the corner at midnight by truck.

( ) 19. Bill's customers were pleased with Bill's job.

( ) 20. Bill saved all the money he earned as a newspaper boy for college expenses.

( ) 21. Sometimes Bill's father helped him send newspapers to people.

( ) 22. Bill was a boy who might enjoy listening to music.

( ) 23. If Bill won a new bike instead of a trip to Europe, he would feel disappointed.

---

Ⅳ、Listen to the passage and fill in the blanks with proper words. （聽短文,用最恰當的填空,每格限填一詞）（共 7 分）

- A newspaper reporter will __24__ different kinds of people in the job.
- A reporter may have a __25__ job after looking for news everywhere for some years.
- A reporter's job ranges from covering a __26__ area to a special one.
- A reporter writes book reviews after reading the __27__ books.
- A reporter always watches movies __28__ movies are on at cinemas.
- A group of tough guys __29__ a reporter's camera when they were taken pictures of 3 years ago.
- A reporter's job is both exciting and dangerous but never ever __30__.

24. _____ 25. _____ 26. _____ 27. _____
28. _____ 29. _____ 30. _____

# 夏朵英文

## 全新英語聽力會考總複習試題

# Unit 12

---

I、Listen and choose the right picture.（根據你所聽到的內容,選出相應的圖片。）（6 分）

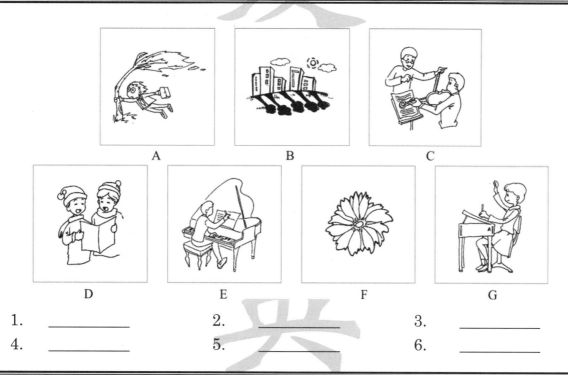

A      B      C

D      E      F      G

1. _____    2. _____    3. _____
4. _____    5. _____    6. _____

---

II、Listen to the dialogue and choose the best answer to the question. （根據你所聽到的對話和問題，選出最恰當的答案。）（10 分）

( ) 7. (A)Go 1 floor higher.      (B)Go 3 floors higher.
        (C)Go 2 floors lower.      (D)Go 3 floors lower.

( ) 8. (A)Having a rest.      (B)Taking a sunbath.
        (C)Collecting shells.      (D)Making sandcastles.

( ) 9. (A)A pet cat.      (B)A naughty kid.
        (C)A friend of theirs.      (D)A pet dog.

( ) 10. (A)Because the forecast tells it to him.
         (B)Because he will have many tests.
         (C)Because it is going to rain.
         (D)Because the boy is poor at all subjects.

( ) 11. (A)3:20.      (B)3:50.      (C)2:45.      (D)3:25.

( ) 12. (A)Toast with jam. (B)Bread with jam.
(C)Bread with butter. (D)Toast with butter.

( ) 13. (A)In a bookstore. (B)In a library.
(C)In the classroom. (D)In a map shop.

( ) 14. (A)Traveling in the world. (B)Their summer holiday.
(C)A romantic country — France. (D)Jobs they do.

( ) 15. (A)Friday. (B)Thursday.
(C)Wednesday. (D)Tuesday.

( ) 16. (A)She went to buy some medicine. (B)She took her mom to hospital.
(C)She planned to miss the lessons. (D)She was badly ill.

---

**Ⅲ、Listen to the passage and tell whether the following statements are true or false.**
（判斷下列句子是否符合你听到的短文內容,符合用 **T** 表示,不符合用 **F** 表示）（7分）

( ) 17. All the Americans think baseball is their national sport.

( ) 18. A baseball game is played by altogether 18 players.

( ) 19. There are five bases for players to run around in a baseball game.

( ) 20. The team can get one point by hitting the ball.

( ) 21. Good baseball players catch the balls better than throw them.

( ) 22. There are few baseball games in summer as the weather is too hot.

( ) 23. A baseball game can take several hours.

---

**Ⅳ、Listen to the passage and fill in the blanks with proper words.**（聽短文,用最恰當的填空,每格限填一詞）（共7分）

● IPF is a great way to learn a new __24__ as well.

● On 7 April, __25__, International Pen Friends was founded in Dublin, Ireland.

● IPF feels like keeping the art of letter writing __26__.

● IPF has __27__ pen friends for more than one and a half million people aged from 7 to 80.

● A member of IPF should give his or her personal __28__.

● The name, the age, the nationality, __29__ and other things are given to IPF.

● This system makes it __30__ for members to choose their pen friends by writing introductory letters to the people.

24. _____  25. _____  26. _____  27. _____

28. _____  29. _____  30. _____

I、Listen and choose the right picture.（根據你所聽到的內容,選出相應的圖片。）（6分）

A          B          C

D          E          F          G

1. _____          2. _____          3. _____
4. _____          5. _____          6. _____

II、Listen to the dialogue and choose the best answer to the question. （根據你所聽到的對話和問題，選出最恰當的答案。）（10分）

（  ）7.　(A)Visit her aunt.　　　　　(B)See her grandma.
　　　　　(C)Watch the show　　　　　(D)Go to the park.

（  ）8.　(A)Math and physics.　　　　(B)Physics and Chinese.
　　　　　(C)English and math.　　　　(D)English and Chinese.

（  ）9.　(A)Next Monday.　　　　　　(B)Next Friday.
　　　　　(C)Next Wednesday.　　　　(D)Next Thursday.

（  ）10.　(A)By metro.　　　　　　　(B)By taxi.
　　　　　　(C)By car.　　　　　　　(D)On foot.

（  ）11.　(A)The woman with long hair is 37 years old.
　　　　　　(B)The woman with short hair is a teacher.
　　　　　　(C)The class teacher of Class Ten has long hair.
　　　　　　(D)The class teacher of Class Four is 37 years old.

( ) 12. (A)In a bookstore. (B)At the bank.
(C)In the post office. (D)In a museum.

( ) 13. (A)13815273749. (B)13817253749.
(C)13817273549. (D)13817273745.

( ) 14. (A)94 points. (B)96 points.
(C)98 points. (D)100 points.

( ) 15. (A)How to study well. (B)Super stars.
(C)A TV program. (D)Daily news.

( ) 16. (A)England. (B)France.
(C)America. (D)Germany.

---

**Ⅲ、Listen to the passage and tell whether the following statements are true or false.**
（判斷下列句子是否符合你听到的短文内容,符合用 **T** 表示,不符合用 **F** 表示）（7分）

( ) 17. A young traveler lost his way on the Alps.

( ) 18. An old man with magic power saved the traveler's life.

( ) 19. The old man used a metal pipe to dig a hole where the seed could be put.

( ) 20. The old man lived alone and wanted to do something useful.

( ) 21. The traveler came to the place again twenty years later.

( ) 22. The wasteland disappeared and the land looked beautiful and smelt nice.

( ) 23. The writer saw the 100,000 trees and was thankful to the old man.

---

**Ⅳ、Listen to the passage and fill in the blanks with proper words.**（聽短文,用最恰當的填空,每格限填一詞）（共7分）

- In Japan, a new electronic __24__ book has appeared.

- The books tell where you are, the history of landmarks and buildings, and the shopping __25__ of the city.

- All the buildings, shops, neon lights and __26__ streets around you make you confused in Japan.

- The electronic book looks like a smart __27__ in appearance.

- Travelers as well as __28__ people can have some fun with the newly-produced book.

- The book is more useful and __29__ than a normal map.

- What the system __30__ is "Anyone, any time, anywhere".

24. _____  25. _____  26. _____  27. _____

28. _____  29. _____  30. _____

# 夏朵英文

## 全新英語聽力會考總複習試題

# Unit 14

---

I、Listen and choose the right picture.（根據你所聽到的內容,選出相應的圖片。）（6分）

A        B        C

D        E        F        G

1. _____　　2. _____　　3. _____

4. _____　　5. _____　　6. _____

---

II、Listen to the dialogue and choose the best answer to the question.（根據你所聽到的對話和問題，選出最恰當的答案。）（10分）

(　) 7.    (A)By plane.    (B)By car.    (C)By train.    (D)By bicycle.

(　) 8.    (A)9 yuan.    (B)5 yuan.    (C)1.5 yuan.    (D)4.5 yuan.

(　) 9.    (A)Jason.    (B)Rose.    (C)Roy.    (D)Jack.

(　) 10.    (A)Ancient Egypt.        (B)Ancient China.

             (C)Ancient Greece.       (D)Ancient Rome.

(　) 11.    (A)To fly kites with Alice.

             (B)To talk over something with friends.

             (C)To go boating with her friends.

             (D)To eat in a restaurant.

(　) 12.    (A)30 min.    (B)35 min.    (C)20 min.    (D)45 min.

( ) 13. (A)Shopping for a hat. (B)Having the hair cut.
(C)Dressing up. (D)Taking a picture.

( ) 14. (A)Because he was not careful enough.
(B)Because he didn't have a good sleep.
(C)Because he didn't have enough exercises.
(D)Because he never put the notes down.

( ) 15. (A)Five o'clock. (B)Half past two.
(C)Three thirty. (D)Four thirty.

( ) 16. (A)The man is the hope for Alice and he will help her.
(B)The man wants Alice to breathe deep to relax.
(C)The man has pity on Alice, but he thinks everything will be better soon.
(D)The man wants Alice never to give up.

Ⅲ、Listen to the passage and tell whether the following statements are true or false. （判断下列句子是否符合你听到的短文内容,符合用 T 表示,不符合用 F 表示）（7分）

( ) 17. A teacher planned to kill President Obama.

( ) 18. The mistake came from one of a math teacher's lessons.

( ) 19. The teacher was arrested and put into prison.

( ) 20. In the lesson, the teacher talked about when and where to stand and aim if shooting Obama with the students.

( ) 21. The students found out the best position in a building to shoot Obama.

( ) 22. The school has decided to have a long talk with the teacher.

( ) 23. The school thinks that there is something wrong with the teacher's expressions.

Ⅳ、Listen to the passage and fill in the blanks with proper words. （聽短文,用最恰當的填空,每格限填一詞）（共7分）

● "Beloved country" is the title of a __24__.

● Ah! Of the motherland, you are the blue sky, I was __25__ in the blue sky on a white cloud;

● Ah! Of the motherland, you are the sea, I am just the __26__ sea spray;

● Ah! Of the motherland, you are the mountains, I am a tall and __27__ tree on the mountain;

● Ah! Of the motherland, you are a road __28__ to the distant, ah, I was walking on this road one of the students to pursue a dream.

- On your 60-year-old birthday, I want you to sing the Ode 60. I wish you will __29__ prosper.

- I want you to light 60 candles, Illuminates every corner of yours; I would also like for you to fly 60 doves of peace, I wish you __30__ peace and happiness ...

24. _____    25. _____    26. _____    27. _____
28. _____    29. _____    30. _____

# 夏朵英文

## 全新英語聽力會考總複習原文及參考答案

# Unit 1

I、Listen and choose the right picture.（根據你所聽到的內容,選出相應的圖片。）(6分)

1. My pen-friend works as a postman and he is hardworking.
   （我的筆友的工作是郵差且他努力工作。）
   答案：(E)

2. Mrs. Wang is not only our Math teacher, but our good friend as well.
   （王太太不只是我們的數學老師，而且也是我們的好朋友。）
   答案：(D)

3. The Teddy Bear is my only friend and I always read books with him.
   （這泰迪熊是我唯一的朋友，我總是和他一起讀書。）
   答案：(A)

4. My father likes to play basketball with me and he looks like my close friend.
   （我父親喜歡和我一起打籃球，他看起來像我親密的朋友。）
   答案：(G)

5. Jason is not my real friend as he cares only for money.
   （傑森不是我真正的朋友因為他只在乎錢。）
   答案：(B)

6. Martin is Kitty's brother and is friendly to his little sister.
   （馬丁是凱悌的哥哥且對他的妹妹很友善。）

答案：(F)

7.　M: Who wrote this letter to you, Alice?（男：這封信是誰寫給妳的，愛麗絲？）

　　W: My pen-pal Mike. He is now like my big brother.（女：我的筆友麥克。他現在就好像我哥哥一樣。）

　　Q: Who is Mike?（問題：麥克是誰？）

　　(A)Alice's cousin.（愛麗絲的表哥。）　　　　　(B)Alice's brother.（愛麗絲的哥哥。）

　　(C)Alice's sister.（愛麗絲的姊姊。）　　　　　(D)Alice's pen-friend.（愛麗絲的筆友。）

　　答案：(D)

8.　M: Lisa, is your pen friend from Japan?（男：莉莎，妳的筆友是來自日本嗎？）

　　W: She stayed in Japan for just several weeks. Now she lives in China. But she is Korean.（女：她只在日本待了幾個星期。現在她住在中國。但她是韓國人。）

　　Q: What is Lisa's pen friend's nationality?（問題：莉莎的筆友是何國籍？）

　　(A)German.（德國。）　　　　　　　　　　　(B)Japanese.（日本。）

　　(C)Korean.（韓國。）　　　　　　　　　　　(D)Chinese.（中國。）

　　答案：(C)

9.　M: I want to borrow this book. It tells us how to write letters.

　　　（男：我想借這本書。它告訴我們如何寫信。）

　　W: So you often write letters?（女：所以你經常寫信嗎？）

　　M: Yes, I have many pen-friends.（男：是的，我有很多筆友。）

　　Q: Where does this dialogue take place?（問題：這段會話在哪裡發生？）

　　(A)In a bookstore.（在一間書店。）　　　　　(B)In a library.（在一間圖書館。）

　　(C)In a hospital.（在一所醫院。）　　　　　(D)In a cinema.（在一間電影院。）

　　答案：(B)

10.　M: Daisy, what is the most important thing for us to remember when we make friends?（男：黛西，我們在交朋友的時候需要記住最重要的是什麼？）

　　W: I think to be honest is quite essential. Do you think so?

　　　（女：我認為誠實是頗重要的。你也這樣想嗎？）

　　M: Yes, I agree. And in my opinion, to be kind and helpful is also important.

　　　（男：是的，我同意。而且在我看來，親切和樂於助人也很重要。）

　　Q: What are they talking about?（問題：他們在聊什麼？）

　　(A)When we need to make friends.（我們何時需要交朋友。）

　　(B)Why we need to make friends.（我們為何需要交朋友。）

　　(C)When to make friends.（交朋友的時機。）

　　(D)How to make friends.（如何交朋友。）

　　答案：(D)

11. M: It is raining outside. Will you still go to the market to shop with your friends?
   （男：外面正下著雨。你仍然會跟妳朋友們去市場購物嗎？）

   W: I'm afraid I will be all wet. So I decide to go shopping tomorrow.
   （女：我恐怕會濕透透。所以我決定明天去購物。）

   M: What a coincidence! There will be special prices on Tuesday. You are so lucky. （男：多麼巧啊！星期二將會有特價。妳真幸運。）

   Q: What day is it today? （問題：今天星期幾？）

   (A)Monday. （星期一。）　　　　　　　(B)Sunday. （星期日。）

   (C)Tuesday. （星期二。）　　　　　　(D)Wednesday. （星期三。）

   答案：(A)

12. M: As we are friends, may I have your e-mail address?
   （男：既然我們是朋友，我可以跟妳要電郵地址嗎？）

   W: OK. It's L-L-O-O-V-V-E-E @ hotmail.com.
   （女：好啊。L-L-O-O-V-V-E-E 小老鼠 hotmail.com.）

   M: Let's keep in touch. （男：讓我們保持聯絡。）

   Q: How will they keep in touch?（問題：他們將如何保持聯絡？）

   (A)By visiting their houses. （去彼此家拜訪。）

   (B)By writing ordinary mails. （寫普通信件。）

   (C)By writing e-mails. （寫電子郵件。）

   (D)By phone. （用電話。）

   答案：(C)

13. M: Excuse me, how can I get to the People's Park?
   （男：不好意思，我要如何去大眾公園？）

   W: I suggest you walk to the nearest underground station. Then you will easily know how to get there.
   （女：我建議你走到最靠近的地鐵站。然後你將很容易得知如何去那裡。）

   M: So, I have to turn left or right? （男：所以，我該轉左邊還是右邊？）

   W: Just walk straight. You will find one within 5 minutes.
   （女：就直走。你將在五分鐘以內找到一個。）

   Q: How will the man go to the nearest station?
   （問題：這位男士將如何去最靠近的車站？）

   (A)By underground. （搭地鐵。）　　　　(B)By taxi. （搭計程車。）

   (C)By bus. （搭巴士。）　　　　　　　(D)On foot. （走路。）

   答案：(D)

14. M: Do you often watch cartoons?（男：妳常常看卡通嗎？）

   W: Cartoons are not my favorite and I only enjoy action movies.
   （女：卡通不是我的最愛，我只愛看動作片。）

   M: I like to watch horror movies and adventure ones.
   （男：我喜歡看恐怖片和冒險片。）

Q: What are the lady's favorite movies?（問題：這位淑女最愛哪種電影？）
(A)Cartoons.（卡通。） (B)Action movies.（動作片。）
(C)Horror movies.（恐怖片。） (D)Adventure movies.（冒險片。）
答案：(B)

15. M: How many friends do you have?（男：妳有多少位朋友？）
　　W: I have so many friends around me.（女：我有那麼多朋友在我身邊。）
　　M: It just means you don't have real friends.
　　　（男：這只表示妳沒有真正的朋友。）
　　Q: What does the man mean?（問題：這位男士的意思是？）
　　(A)It's impossible to make real friends with so many people.
　　　（和那麼多人成為真正的朋友是不可能的。）
　　(B)In fact, the woman has no friends around her.
　　　（事實上，這位女士沒有朋友在她身邊。）
　　(C)The woman is telling a lie and she is dishonest.（這位女士說謊，她不誠實。）
　　(D)The man wants to tell the woman not to make many friends.
　　　（這位男士想要告訴這位女士不要交很多朋友。）
　　答案：(A)

16. W: Mike, when will the film begin?（女：麥克，電影何時將會開始？）
　　M: Let me check the ticket. It will begin at 8.
　　　（男：讓我查看電影票。它將在八點開始。）
　　W: Can we meet at the entrance at 7:55?
　　　（女：我們可以七點五十五分在入口見面嗎？）
　　M: Why not ten minutes earlier? We can buy some snacks there.
　　　（男：為何不提早十分鐘？我們可以在那裡買些點心。）
　　W: Good idea! See you soon.（女：好主意！待會見。）
　　Q: When will they meet at the entrance?（問題：他們將幾點在入口見面？）
　　(A)At 8.（八點整） (B)At 7:45.（七點四十五分）
　　(C)At 7:55.（七點五十五分） (D)At 8:05.（八點五分）
　　答案：(B)

Ⅲ、Listen to the passage and tell whether the following statements are true or false.
（判斷下列句子是否符合你聽到的短文內容,符合用 T 表示,不符合用 F 表示）(7 分)

　　As a human being, one can hardly do without a friend, for life without friends will be a lonely journey in the dark sea or one in the desert. Truly, a friend gives out light and warmth like a lamp. For this reason, I have always felt it a lucky time if a friend comes to me in my sadness, cheer me up in my low spirits, or share my happiness with me. It is wonderful, too, to feel that someone is standing by me and ready to provide help and encouragement during my growth.

身為人類，一個人幾乎不能沒有朋友，因為沒有朋友的人生將會是在黑暗的海洋上或是沙漠中一個孤單的旅程。真的，一位朋友帶來如同一盞燈的光和溫暖。因此，如果一個朋友在我悲傷時來看我，在我心情沮喪時來鼓勵我，或者和我分享我的快樂，我總是感到那是幸運的時光。在我的成長中感受到某人站在我身邊準備好提供幫助和鼓勵，也是很棒的。

A real friend is considered even more precious than a priceless pearl or an expensive house. The old saying "A friend in need is a friend indeed" has told us what true friends mean.

一個真正的朋友被視為比一顆無價的珍珠或一幢昂貴的房子還要珍貴。一句古老諺語「患難見真情」告訴我們真朋友的意義。

Still, it is natural that different people have different ideas in making friends. Some think it important to make friends with whom they may share the same interests or hobbies with. Others are going to find friends so as to get some favors or special help. And I am one of those who think very little of similarity or position or power. As long as a person is warm-hearted, selfless, honest, open-minded, but not cruel, cold, shortsighted nor narrow-minded, I am willing to make friends with him or her, give my support and help, and remain unchanged to him or her all my life.

然而，自然地，不同的人對交朋友有不同的想法。有些人認為和可以分享共同興趣或嗜好的人交朋友是重要的。其他人則尋找些可以得到益處或特別幫助的朋友。而我是那些對身分或地位或權力想得很少的人當中的一個。只要這個人有溫暖的心、無私、誠實、思想開放，但不無情、冷漠、短視或思想狹隘，我就很願意和他或她交朋友，提供我的支持和幫助，且一輩子對他或她維持不變。

17. Human beings can't do without friends. （人類不能沒朋友。）
    答案：(T 對)

18. The writer doesn't want her friends to come to her when she is very sad.
    （筆者不想要她的朋友在她悲傷時來看她。）
    答案：(F 錯)

19. According to the writer, a real friend is the same as a precious pearl.
    （根據筆者，一個真正的朋友就像一顆珍貴的珍珠。）
    答案：(F 錯)

20. To have the same hobbies or interests is the first thing that people consider when they make friends.
    （擁有相同的嗜好或興趣是人們交朋友時首先考慮的。）
    答案：(F 錯)

21. The writer wants to make friends with those who have enough power.
    （筆者想要和有足夠權力的人們交朋友。）

答案：(F 錯)

22. The writer doesn't want to make friends with people who wear glasses.
（筆者不想要和戴眼鏡的人們交朋友。）
答案：(F 錯)

23. The support the writer gives to her friend will never change all her life.
（筆者對她朋友提供的支持將一輩子都不改變。）
答案：(T 對)

---

**IV、Listen to the passage and fill in the blanks with proper words.**（聽短文,用最恰當的填空,每格限填一詞）（共 7 分）

---

I have a pen-pal called John from the United States. He is a middle school student of Grade 2. He is good at math and physics. Of course, he is a top student in his class. When I started to write to him, he invited me to teach him Chinese. It seems that he has lots of interests and he plans to learn everything strange to him. In his letter, he tells me many stories in his country, his school and his family as well. Anyway, he is a good boy. I love him and like to make friends with him. I hope that he will come to China some day in the future. Then, we can communicate with each other and have a good time together.

我有位筆友叫約翰，來自美國。他是一名中學二年級的學生。他在數學和物理方面很拿手。當然，他在他的班上名列前茅。當我開始寫信給他，他請我教他中文。他似乎有很多興趣並且計畫學習任何對他來說新奇的東西。在他的信中，他告訴我很多他的國家、他的學校還有他的家庭的故事。不管怎麼說，他是個好孩子。我愛他並且想和他做朋友。我希望他未來有一天會來到中國。那時，我們可以互相溝通並一起玩樂。

---

- The nationality of the pen-friend is __24__.
  （該筆友的國籍是美國。）
- Now he studies in Grade __25__ in a Junior High School.
  （目前他就讀國中的二年級。）
- The subjects he does well in are __26__ and math.
  （他拿手的科目是物理和數學。）
- The pen-friend __27__ me to teach him Chinese at the beginning.
  （該筆友最初請我教他中文。）
- He seems to have lots of __28__.
  （他似乎有很多興趣。）
- In his letters, he shares with me many __29__ in his country.
  （在他的信中，他和我分享很多他國家的故事。）
- I hope to meet him in China so that we can __30__ with each other better.
  （我希望和他在中國見面這樣我們可以彼此溝通得更好。）

24. 答案：American
25. 答案：Two／2
26. 答案：physics
27. 答案：invited
28. 答案：interests
29. 答案：stories
30. 答案：communicate

# 夏朵英文

## 全新英語聽力會考總複習原文及參考答案

# Unit 2

I、Listen and choose the right picture.（根據你所聽到的內容,選出相應的圖片。）（6 分）

1. Mary hurried to school and she decided to work harder than before.
   （瑪莉趕忙到學校且她決定要比以前更用功。）
   答案：(E)

2. Stockton worked as a basketball player and he practiced a lot.
   （斯托克頓的工作是籃球選手，他勤奮練習。）
   答案：(A)

3. The boy's mother told him to spend more time on study in the letter.
   （這位男孩的母親在信中要他多花時間在學業上。）
   答案：(B)

4. Jerry drove his toy car happily and he had much fun yesterday afternoon.
   （昨天下午傑瑞快樂地開著他的玩具車玩得很開心。）
   答案：(D)

5. After dinner, Tim often watches TV with his mother as a way of relaxing.
   （晚餐後，湯姆經常和他的母親一起看電視當作一種放鬆的方法。）
   答案：(F)

6.  If I want to serve as a pilot, I have to protect my eyes.
    （如果我想要擔任飛行員，我必須保護我的眼睛。）
    答案：(C)

---

**II、Listen to the dialogue and choose the best answer to the question.** （根據你所聽到的對話和問題，選出最恰當的答案。）（10 分）

7.  W: What do you do, Mike? （女：你是做什麼的，麥克？）
    M: I help make sick people better. （男：我幫助生病的人好起來。）
    W: What a nice job! I wish you success. （女：多好的工作啊！我祝你成功。）
    Q: What is Mike? （問題：麥克的職業是？）
    (A)A policeman. （一位警察）　　(B)A nurse. （一位護士）
    (C)A secretary. （一位秘書）　　(D)A doctor. （一位醫師）
    答案：(B)

8.  W: When do you leave for work every day? （女：你每天幾點出門上班？）
    M: Normally I leave home at 8:20 and start my work from 9 o'clock. But on rainy days, I will leave home half an hour earlier. （男：正常來說我八點二十分離開家然後九點開始工作。但是在雨天，我會提早半小時出門。）
    Q: If today is rainy, when will the man leave home for work?
    （問題：如果今天下雨，這位男士將幾點出門上班？）
    (A)At 9 o'clock. （九點鐘）　　(B)At 8:30. （八點三十分）
    (C)At 8:20. （八點二十分）　　(D)At 7:50. （七點五十分）
    答案：(D)

9.  W: Come on. There are so many books that are waiting for you to be put back.
    （女：拜託。有那麼多的書等你把它們放回去。）
    M: How strange people are! Why didn't they buy these copies they picked out?
    （男：這些人真奇怪！為什麼他們不買他們抽出來的這些書呢？）
    W: As I know, many people look on our place as a free library.
    （女：據我所知，很多人把我們這地方視為免費圖書館。）
    Q: Where do the two persons work? （問題：這兩個人在哪裡工作？）
    (A)In a library. （在一間圖書館）　　(B)In a post office. （在一間郵局）
    (C)In a bookstore. （在一間書店）　　(D)At the airport. （在一座機場）
    答案：(C)

10. W: Can you play any musical instrument? （女：你會彈奏任何樂器嗎？）
    M: I can play the piano well, but I don't know anything about guitar.
    （男：我鋼琴彈得滿好的，但是我對吉他一無所知。）
    W: Don't worry. Maybe I can be your instructor.
    （女：別擔心。或許我可以當你的指導員。）
    Q: What musical instrument is the woman good at playing?

（問題：這位女士拿手的樂器是什麼？）
(A)The guitar.（吉他）　　　　　(B)The piano.（鋼琴）
(C)The violin.（小提琴）　　　　(D)The drum.（鼓）
答案：(A)

11. W: How can I deal with my baby when she is crying?
　　（女：當我的嬰兒在哭的時候我該把他怎麼辦呢？）
　M: A doll with beautiful clothes may be a good choice.
　　（男：一個穿著漂亮服裝的洋娃娃可能是個好選擇。）
　Q: What does the man mean?（問題：這位男士的意思是？）
　(A)Buying some new clothes will make babies smile.
　　（買些新衣服將會使嬰兒們微笑。）
　(B)Dressing babies the clothes they like will make them smile.
　　（給嬰兒穿上他們喜歡的衣服將會使他們微笑。）
　(C)Showing lovely dolls will make babies smile.
　　（給嬰兒們看可愛的娃娃會讓他們微笑。）
　(D)Dressing babies up like dolls will make them smile.
　　（把嬰兒穿得像娃娃會讓他們微笑。）
　答案：(C)

12. W: I have no idea why teachers are so busy.
　　（女：我真不知道為何老師們如此忙碌。）
　M: Everyone will be busy if he or she puts his / her heart into the job.
　　（男：如果他或她全心貫注於工作都會忙碌。）
　W: Now I know why I am not busy at all.（女：現在我知道為何我一點都不忙了。）
　Q: What can we learn from the dialogue?（問題：從這段對話我們可以得知？）
　(A)The girl doesn't know her teachers.（這位女孩不認識她的老師們。）
　(B)The boy thinks nobody is busy.（這位男孩認為沒有人是忙碌的。）
　(C)The girl isn't hard working.（這位女孩不勤奮。）
　(D)The boy doesn't agree with the girl.（這位男孩不同意這位女孩所說。）
　答案：(C)

13. W: What's wrong with you?（女：你怎麼了？）
　M: I have a stomach-ache. I always feel like that.
　　（男：我胃痛。我總是有這種感覺。）
　W: Do you often forget your breakfast?（女：你常常忘記吃早餐嗎？）
　M: Never ever. But I enjoy only spicy food.
　　（男：從來沒有。但我只喜歡吃辣的食物。）
　W: Is it the cause?（女：是這個原因嗎？）
　M: I'm afraid it is. I will eat more fruits.（男：我恐怕是的。我將會多吃點水果。）
　Q: What does the man think is the reason for his stomach-ache?
　　（問題：這位男士認為他胃痛的原因是什麼？）

(A)Eating much spicy food.（吃太多辣的食物。）

(B)Not taking medicine.（不吃藥。）

(C)Not eating breakfast regularly.（沒有正常地吃早餐。）

(D)Enjoy too many fruits.（享用太多水果。）

答案：(A)

14. W: Lucy is a good secretary and she works hard.
    （女：露西是個好秘書且工作勤奮。）

    M: Thank you. I am proud of my wife. But she tells me that she learns a lot from your husband.
    （男：謝謝。我為我妻子感到驕傲。但是她告訴我她從妳先生那邊學到很多。）

    W: My husband is work alcoholic.（女：我先生是個工作狂。）

    Q: What does the woman mean?（問題：這位女士的意思是？）

    (A)Lucy works harder than her husband.（露西比她先生工作更勤奮。）

    (B)Her husband works very hard.（她先生工作很勤奮。）

    (C)Her husband likes drinking.（她先生喜歡喝酒。）

    (D)She works harder than her husband.（她比她先生工作更勤奮。）

    答案：(B)

15. W: Where are you from?（女：你來自哪裡？）

    M: I am from the United Kingdom and work in Canada.
    （男：我來自英國而在加拿大工作。）

    W: Is this your first time to visit Shanghai?（女：這是你第一次造訪上海嗎？）

    M: Yes, I am on my holiday.（男：是的，我正在度假中。）

    Q: Which country does the man come from?（問題：這位男士來自哪個國家？）

    (A)Shanghai.（上海）　　　　　　　(B)China.（中國）

    (C)Canada.（加拿大）　　　　　　　(D)Britain.（英國）

    答案：(D)

16. W: Why are you tired of playing computer games, Mike?
    （女：你為什麼厭倦玩電腦遊戲了，麥可？）

    M: My English score is falling down so quickly that I have to catch up.
    （男：我的英語成績下降得那麼快以至於我必須趕上進度。）

    W: Really? I will tell our mother about it. I am sure she will be happy as well.
    （女：真的？我會把此事告訴我們的母親。我確定她也會很高興。）

    Q: Who is the woman?（問題：這位女士是誰？）

    (A)Mike's mother.（麥可的母親）　　(B)Mike's teacher.（麥可的老師）

    (C)Mike's sister.（麥可的姊妹）　　(D)Mike's classmate.（麥可的同學）

    答案：(C)

---

Ⅲ、Listen to the passage and tell whether the following statements are true or false.
（判斷下列句子是否符合你聽到的短文內容，符合用 T 表示，不符合用 F 表示）(7分)

There lived a group of monkeys in a forest. Every day, when the sun rose they went out finding food, and came back for rest at sunset. Life was simple and happy.

在一座森林裡住著一群猴子。每天，當太陽升起牠們就出去找食物，然後夕陽西下時回來休息。生活是單純而快樂的。

One day, monkey David found a watch on a rock, which was dropped by a traveler when traveling in the forest. David was so clever that it worked out how to use the watch soon. News traveled very fast. All monkeys then heard about the watch and would come to ask David for the time. They even decided that David was the timetable maker of their group. All monkeys believed David and finally David became the Monkey King.

有一天，猴子大衛在一塊岩石上找到一隻錶，這是一位旅人在森林裡旅行時掉下的。大衛是那麼地聰明很快就弄清楚了怎麼使用這隻錶。消息傳得很快。全部的猴子都聽說了關於錶的事並且會來向大衛問時間。牠們甚至決定了大衛當牠們群體中的時間表製作者。全部的猴子們相信大衛並且最後大衛成為了猴子王。

David liked the watch so much. So it went around every day in the forest, hoping to pick up more watches. In return, it got the second watch, then the third one.

大衛是那麼地喜歡這隻錶。所以牠每天在森林裡到處走，希望撿到更多錶。如願地，牠得到了第二隻錶，然後第三隻。

But David had a new trouble then: each watch told a different time. Which was the right one? David got puzzled. When other monkeys came to ask about the time, David could not answer, therefore work and rest for monkeys got out of order. It wasn't long before monkeys drove David away. David became a poor monkey and died soon.

但是大衛此時有了新的麻煩：每隻錶顯示的時間都不一樣。哪個才是正確的？大衛困惑了。當其牠的猴子來向牠問時間，大衛無法回答，因此猴子們的工作和休息都失去了規律。不久後猴子們把大衛逼走了。大衛變成一隻可憐的猴子且很快就死了。

17. The group of monkeys lived an exciting and rich life in a forest.
（這群猴子在森林裡過著刺激精彩且豐富的生活。）
答案：(F 錯)

18. Monkey David stole a watch from a traveler.
（猴子大衛從一位旅人處偷了一隻錶。）
答案：(F 錯)

19. No monkeys knew how to use the watch and they threw it away.
（沒有猴子知道如何使用這隻錶而牠們把它給丟了。）
答案：(F 錯)

20. The watch helped David to be the king of the group.
（這隻錶幫助大衛成為群體中的王。）

答案：(T 對)

21. David could tell more accurate time with the help of more watches.
（大衛可藉著更多錶的幫助而告知更精確的時間。）

答案：(F 錯)

22. Other monkeys were always satisfied with David's job.
（其他猴子總是對大衛的工作感到滿意。）

答案：(F 錯)

23. From the story, we can conclude that watches are not as helpful as the sun.
（從這個故事，我們可以得到個結論是錶不如太陽那麼有助益。）

答案：(F 錯)

---

**IV、Listen to the passage and fill in the blanks with proper words.**（聽短文,用最恰當的填空,每格限填一詞）（共 7 分）

---

M: It's time to graduate and it's time to find a job. Susan, why do we need to find a job?
（男：是畢業的時候也是找個工作的時候了。蘇珊，為什麼我們需要找工作？）

W: It is because we need money to live. We need money for food and clothes and to pay for houses. We need money for many different things, and only when we work can we earn money. And work can also help us feel that we are useful. （女：因為我們需要錢來生活。我們需要錢買食物和衣服還有支付房子。我們需要錢買不同的東西，而唯有工作可以讓我們賺錢。且工作也可以幫助我們感到自己有用。）

M: But you know it's hard for a new graduate to find a good job right now.
（男：但是妳知道對一個剛畢業的人來說現在很難找到工作。）

W: Yes, it is really hard. But you must believe that you will find a suitable job finally. When you work, you can accumulate a lot of experience. Besides, you need to learn a lot of things while you are working.
（女：是的，真的很難。但是你必須相信你終究會找到個適合的工作。當你工作時，你可以累積很多經驗。此外，當你在工作時你需要學習很多東西。）

M: I've been fed up with study. （男：我對學習已經膩了。）

W: But whether you like it or not, there's a trend of life-long study to make sure that we can keep ourselves up with the high developing society. And you need to accept this concept positively.
（女：但無論你喜不喜歡，有個終生學習的趨勢好確保我們可以讓自己跟上高度發展的社會。並且你必須積極地接受這個概念。）

M: Oh, my god. Why are there still so many things to learn after graduation?
（男：噢，我的天。為什麼在畢業之後還有那麼多東西要學？）

W: You have no choice, so you'd better adjust your thoughts to be ready to learn anything at any time.
（女：你別無選擇，所以你最好調整你的想法準備好在任何時候學習任何東西。）

- We need money for __24__ and food and to pay for houses.
  （我們需要錢買衣服和食物還有支付房子。）
- Work can help us feel that we are __25__ as well.
  （工作也可以幫助我們感到我們是有用的。）
- It's hard for a new __26__ to find a good job immediately.
  （對剛畢業的新鮮人來說很難立即找到工作。）
- When you work, you can gather a lot of __27__ for future jobs.
  （當你工作，你可以為將來的工作收集很多經驗。）
- __28__ study is a trend to make sure that we can keep ourselves up with the high developing society.
  （終生學習是個趨勢好確保我們可以讓自己跟上高度發展的社會。）
- We have no __29__ but to adjust our thoughts to be ready to learn anything at any time.
  （我們別無選擇只能調整自己的想法準備好在任何時候學習任何東西。）
- Susan has a right attitude (態度) towards __30__.
  （蘇珊對工作有正確的態度。）

24. 答案：clothes（衣服）
25. 答案：useful（有用的）
26. 答案：graduate（畢業生）
27. 答案：experience（經驗）
28. 答案：Life-long（終生）
29. 答案：choice（選擇）
30. 答案：work（工作）

# 夏朵英文

## 全新英語聽力會考總複習原文及參考答案

# Unit 3

I、Listen and choose the right picture.（根據你所聽到的內容,選出相應的圖片。）（6 分）

A      B      C

D      E      F      G

1. Mr. Ding helped his students to work out the difficult problems.
   （丁先生幫助他的學生們解困難的問題。）
   答案：(B)

2. We are a big family and we can bravely deal with any trouble.
   （我們是個大家庭，我們可以勇敢地處理任何麻煩。）
   答案：(D)

3. That old man is in trouble now. Let's help him as soon as possible.
   （這老人正陷入麻煩中。讓我們盡快幫助他吧。）
   答案：(G)

4. Although Sam had a sore throat, he could still sing wonderful songs for us.
   （雖然山姆喉嚨痛，他仍然可以為我們唱美妙的歌曲。）
   答案：(A)

5. The baby had trouble in walking. So he tried his best to crawl on the ground.
   （這嬰兒有行走上的困難。所以他盡力在地上爬。）
   答案：(C)

6. Jack is good at Chinese and he has written many excellent compositions.

（傑克中文方面很拿手，他寫了很多傑出的文章。）

答案：(E)

---

Ⅱ、Listen to the dialogue and choose the best answer to the question. （根據你所聽到的對話和問題，選出最恰當的答案。）（10分）

7. M: How can I work out this math problem?（男：我們要怎麼計算出這數學題？）

   W: Why not review the last Unit once more? You will find the solution.

   （女：為何不再一次複習上個單元的講解？你將會找到解決方法。）

   M: I got it. Thank you.（男：我懂了。謝謝。）

   Q: What does the girl mean?（問題：這位女孩的意思是？）

   (A)They met with the same problem in the last Unit.

   （他們在上個單元遇到同樣的問題。）

   (B)The boy can find the solution on the last page of a book.

   （這位男孩可以在書的最後一頁找到解決方法。）

   (C)The boy wanted the girl to do more revision.

   （這位男孩希望這位女孩做更多複習。）

   (D)The girl didn't know the solution at all.（這位女孩完全不知道解決方法。）

   答案：(A)

8. M: What's the matter with Alice?（男：愛莉絲是怎麼了？）

   W: She was knocked down by a fat boy and her head was injured.

   （女：她被一位胖男孩撞倒，她的頭受傷了。）

   M: Let's go to the clinic to help.（男：讓我們去診所幫忙吧。）

   Q: What happened to Alice?（問題：愛莉絲發生了什麼事？）

   (A)She became too fat.（她變得太胖了。）

   (B)She fell off her bike.（她騎單車跌下來了。）

   (C)Her leg was injured.（她的腿受傷了。）

   (D)A boy knocked her down.（一位男孩把她撞倒了。）

   答案：(D)

9. M: Mrs. Wang, can you describe the robber?

   （男：王太太，您可以敘述一下這個搶匪嗎？）

   W: He looks young and wears a red hat and a blue coat. The color of his trousers
   is white and the shoes are black.（女：他看起來頗年輕戴著一頂紅帽子穿藍外
   套。他的長褲的顏色是白色而鞋子是黑色。）

   Q: What color is the robber's coat?（問題：這搶劫犯的外套是什麼顏色？）

   (A)Red.（紅色）　　　(B)White.（白色）　(C)Blue.（藍色）　(D)Black.（黑色）

   答案：(C)

10. M: Martin is crying. What's up?（男：馬丁正在哭。怎麼回事？）

    W: He didn't finish his dish and just wanted to play the computer games.

（女：他沒有吃完他的餐而只想玩電腦遊戲。）

M: That's terrible. Let him be.（男：那糟透了。隨便他。）

Q: What happened to Martin?（問題：馬丁發生了什麼事？）

(A)He didn't eat up his dinner.（他沒有吃完他的晚餐。）

(B)He played computer games for too long.（他玩了太久的電腦遊戲。）

(C)He was sick.（他生病了。）

(D)He didn't wash his dish.（他沒有洗他的盤子。）

答案：(A)

11. M: I want to visit the museum. How can I get the tickets?

（男：我想要參觀博物館。我如何取得門票呢？）

W: You have to wait at the entrance to the museum and the staff will give you the tickets.（女：你必須在博物館入口等，然後工作人員會給你票。）

Q: What are they talking about?（問題：他們在談論什麼？）

(A)Which museum to visit.（要參觀哪一間博物館。）

(B)How to get tickets.（如何取得門票。）

(C)Where the entrance to the museum is.（這間博物館的入口在哪裡。）

(D)When to see the museum.（什麼時候去參觀這間博物館。）

答案：(B)

12. M: The apartment in Shanghai is too expensive. How can I afford it?

（男：在上海的公寓太貴了。我怎麼能負擔得起？）

W: Why not get the loan from the bank? It will be helpful.

（女：為何不向銀行貸款？它會有幫助的。）

Q: What does the woman suggest the man do?

（問題：這位女士建議這位男士做什麼？）

(A)The man should not buy the apartment.（這位男士不應該買公寓。）

(B)The man should save money in the bank.（這位男士應該把錢存在銀行。）

(C)The man should sell all his belongings.（這位男士應該賣掉他所有的物品。）

(D)The man should borrow money from the bank.（這位男士應該向銀行借錢。）

答案：(D)

13. M: Have you ever been to the new Bund? It's amazing.

（男：妳有去過新外灘嗎？很棒喔。）

W: Of course. Now I am waiting for a third time. Will you go with me?

（女：當然。現在我在等著去第三次。你要跟我去嗎？）

Q: How many times has the lady been to the new Bund?

（問題：這位淑女去新外灘幾次了？）

(A)Once.（一次）　　　　　　　　(B)Twice.（兩次）

(C)Three times.（三次）　　　　　(D)Never.（從未）

答案：(B)

14. M: What is Jane doing now? I can't find her in the classroom.

（男：珍現在正在做什麼？我在教室找不到她。）

W: She is practicing dancing with Mike in the art room.

（女：她正在藝術室和麥克一起練習跳舞。）

M: How about Alice? Is she dancing with them?

（男：那愛莉絲呢？她在和他們一起跳舞嗎？）

W: Alice hates dancing. She is reading in the library.

（女：愛莉絲討厭跳舞。她在圖書館讀書。）

Q: Where can we find Mike?（問題：我們可以在哪裡找到麥克？）

(A)In the library.（在圖書館。）　　(B)In the classroom.（在教室。）

(C)In the art room.（在美術室。）　　(D)At home.（在家。）

答案：(C)

15. M: What will the weather be like tomorrow? I plan to go shopping with my friend.（男：明天的天氣會是怎樣呢？我計劃和我朋友一起去購物。）

W: The forecast says that it will be raining from tonight till next morning and be cloudy in the afternoon. At night, a heavy fog will be around us.（女：氣象預測說從今晚到明早會下雨，下午多雲。晚上，一陣濃霧會圍繞著我們。）

M: I see. I will go outside as soon as the rain stops.

（男：我明白了。雨一停我就會出門去。）

Q: What will the weather be like tomorrow night?

（問題：明天晚上的天氣會是怎樣？）

(A)Fine.（好天氣）　　(B)Cloudy.（多雲）

(C)Rainy.（下雨）　　(D)Foggy.（多霧）

答案：(D)

16. M: I want to change a computer. Can you give me some advice?

（男：我想要換電腦。妳可以給我一些建議嗎？）

W: You can buy a SONY computer. It is fashionable.

（女：你可以買一台索尼的電腦。它很時尚。）

M: I'm worried about its speed.（男：我擔心它的速度耶。）

W: An APPLE computer has high speed. I think you will like the brand.

（女：蘋果電腦速度快。我想你會喜歡這個品牌。）

M: But I am not familiar with its system.（男：但是我不熟悉它的系統耶。）

W: You will soon get used to it over time.（女：隨著時間你很快就會習慣的。）

Q: Which statement is true about the SONY computer?

（問題：關於索尼電腦的敘述何者為真？）

(A)It has a new system.（它有新的系統）

(B)It has high speed.（它有高速度）

(C)It's fashionable.（它很時尚）

(D)It's cheap.（它便宜）

答案：(C)

Ability is one thing while success is another.

能力是一回事而成功又是另一回事。

When Joe Cole was a teenager, he was regarded as the boy talent of English football and built up a career that many footballers can only dream of. However, it seems that his early promise has never been truly realized.

當喬柯爾還是個青少年,他被視為英國足球的神童且打造了一個很多足球員夢寐以求的生涯。然而,似乎他的青年希望從未真正被實現。

At the 2010 World Cup, 28-year-old Cole only made just two appearances as a player beside the field. In July 2010 Cole moved to a new team and tried to begin a new start in his career.

在 2010 世界盃,二十八歲的柯爾只以場邊球員上場了兩次。2010 年七月柯爾轉移到一個新球隊並且試著在他的事業生涯開始一個新起點。

Keith Blunt is Cole's coach and also thinks how talented the young Cole was, believing this is an opportunity for Cole to be successful.

基斯布朗特是柯爾的教練也認為年輕的柯爾是多麼有天賦,相信這是柯爾成功的一個機會。

Cole's former teammate Steve, who played with Cole in his old team from 1998 to 2003, also says Cole's move to the new team is the right thing for him. He thinks the reason for Cole not shining as brightly as he might have in the past, is that he wasn't given the right role in the old team.

柯爾的前隊友史提夫,從 1998 到 2003 年在柯爾的老球隊一起踢球,也說柯爾轉移到新球隊對他來說是正確的。他認為柯爾沒有像以前那麼閃亮地大放異彩,是因為他在老球隊沒有被給予正確的角色。

17. Joe Cole is a basketball player and he is talented.
（喬柯爾是一位籃球員並且他很有天賦。）
答案：(F 錯)

18. Joe Cole performed wonderfully at the 2010 World Cup.
（喬柯爾在2012的世界盃表現很出色。）
答案：(F 錯)

19. Cole's coach doesn't think it wise for Cole to change a team.
（柯爾的教練不認為柯爾轉球隊是明智的。）
答案：(F 錯)

20. Steve and Cole played in one team for nearly 3 years.
（史提夫和柯爾在同一個球隊踢了將近三年。）
答案：(F 錯)

21. Steve thinks the reason why Cole isn't successful is that he doesn't work hard.
（史提夫認為柯爾不成功的原因是他沒有努力。）

答案：(F 錯)

22. The old team didn't give Joe Cole the right role.
（老球隊沒有給喬柯爾正確的角色。）

答案：(T 對)

23. If a person has ability, he or she will always succeed.
（如果一個人有能力，他或她總是會成功。）

答案：(F 錯)

---

**IV、Listen to the passage and fill in the blanks with proper words.**（聽短文,用最恰當的填空,每格限填一詞）（共 7 分）

Ladies and gentlemen,

各位女士先生，

Good afternoon! I'm very glad to stand here and give you a short speech. Today my topic is "To be a giver rather than a taker".

午安！我很高興站在這裡為您們做個簡短的演講。今天我的主題是「當個施予者而非受惠者」。

In modern society, more and more people become greedy and selfish. They take others' hard work for granted instead of running after something fairly. They always want to get everything they want but do nothing for it. Now, as it is known to us, some children always take their parents' love naturally. And they think their parents should give them everything they want. So more and more takers are found in our society. More seriously, this situation has a bad effect on our living.

在現代化的社會，越來越多的人們變得貪婪和自私。他們把其他人的努力當作理所當然而不去公平地追求什麼。他們總是想要得到他們想要的一切但是什麼也不付出。現在，如同我們所知道的，有些孩童總是理所當然的接受父母的愛。且他們認為他們的父母應該給他們一切他們想要的。所以在我們的社會裡出現了越來越多的受惠者。更嚴重地，這個狀況對我們的生活有壞的影響。

Now, we believe everyone should pay attention to this social situation. At the same time, we should know: to be a giver doesn't mean that you shouldn't take anything, but you should balance taking with giving; to be a giver doesn't mean that you should give all the things you have but you should help the others who are in trouble; also, to be a giver doesn't mean that you shouldn't ask for material enjoyment, but you should gain it in a right and fair way.

現在，我們相信每個人應該關注這個社會狀況。而同時，我們應該知道：當一個施予者並不意味著你不應該取得任何東西，而是你應該以施予來平衡取用；當一個施予者並不意味著你應該把你的所有都給出去，而是你應該幫助身陷麻煩的其他人；還有，當一個施予者並不意味著你不應該要求物質上的享樂，而是你應該以正確公平的方法獲得它。

So, let's learn to be a giver rather than a taker. Only in this way can we get more happiness from living. And only in this way can the society become more and more harmonious. That's my speech. Thanks for your listening.

所以，讓我們學習當個施予者而非取用者。唯有如此我們可以從生活中得到更多快樂。且唯有如此社會可以變得越來越和諧。以上是我的演講。謝謝各位聆聽。

● The man feels very glad to stand here and give people a short __24__.
（這位男士感到很高興站在這裡為大家做個簡短演講。）

● The man thinks some takers take others' hard work for granted instead of running after something __25__.
（這位男士認為有些受惠者把別人的努力當作理所當然而不去公平地追求什麼。）

● Because of several reasons, more and more takers are __26__ in our society.
（因為幾個原因，在我們的社會出現越來越多取用者。）

● A giver should __27__ taking with giving.
（一位施予者應該以施予來平衡取用。）

● A giver should help the others who are in __28__.
（一位施予者應該幫助在麻煩中的其他人。）

● To be a giver doesn't mean that you shouldn't ask for material __29__.
（當一位施予者並不意味著你不應要求物質上的享樂。）

● We can get __30__ from living in the way of learning to be a good giver.
（我們可以學習當個好施予者這個方法從生活中得到快樂。）

24. 答案：speech（演講）
25. 答案：fairly（公平地）
26. 答案：found（被發現）
27. 答案：balance（平衡）
28. 答案：trouble（麻煩）
29. 答案：enjoyment（享樂）
30. 答案：happiness（快樂）

# 夏朵英文

## 全新英語聽力會考總複習原文及參考答案

# Unit 4

---

**Ⅰ、Listen and choose the right picture.** (根據你聽到的內容,選出相應的圖片。)(6分)

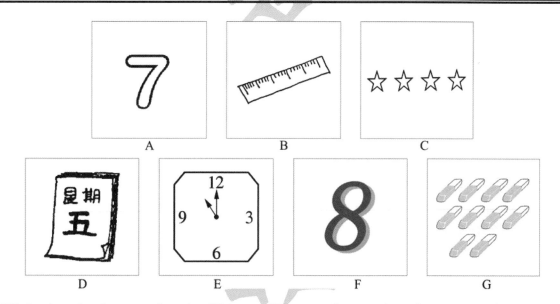

1. Eight is a lucky number in China while maybe not in other countries.
   （八在中國是個幸運數字然而在其他國家就未必。）
   答案：(F)

2. Yesterday we stayed in a four-star hotel and the service was nice.
   （昨天我們住宿在一間四星旅館,服務很好。）
   答案：(C)

3. If we add two rubbers to eight, how many on earth can we get finally?
   （如果我們將八個橡皮擦加上兩個,我們到底最後會有幾個?）
   答案：(G)

4. It's eleven o'clock sharp and lunch will be ready soon.
   （現在十一點整,午餐很快就會準備好。）
   答案：(E)

5. Rulers are used to tell the length of objects. (尺是被用來測知物體的長度。)
   答案：(B)

6. We often eat out on Friday night and attend some evening clubs.
   （我們常常星期五晚上出去外面吃並去參加一些夜間俱樂部。）
   答案：(D)

7.　W: How many students in your class will take part in the Physics Competition?
　　　（女：你的班上有多少位學生會去參加體能競賽？）

　　M: Two fifths of the students in my class will join in the contest.
　　　（男：我們班五分之二的學生會加入比賽。）

　　W: But what's the population of your class?（女：但是你班上人數是多少？）

　　M: Twenty two girls and eighteen boys in all.
　　　（男：總共二十二位女孩和十八位男孩。）

　　Q: How many students in the boy's class will take part in the Physics Competition?（問題：這位男孩的班上多少人會參加體能競賽。）

　　(A)16.　　　　　　(B)40.　　　　　　(C)22.　　　　　　(D)18.

　　答案：(A)

8.　W: When on earth does the plane take off for Paris? I miss my boyfriend.
　　　（女：到底飛機何時才會起飛去巴黎呢？我想念我男朋友。）

　　M: The plane has been delayed for three hours. I was told that we could take off in half an hour.
　　　（男：這班飛機延遲了三小時。我被告知我們將可在半小時後起飛。）

　　W: That means the plane leaves at eleven twenty! I can't believe my ears.
　　　（女：意思是說這班飛機十一點二十分出發！我不能相信我的耳朵。）

　　Q: What time is it now?（問題：現在的時間是？）

　　(A)7:50.　　　　　　(B)10:50.　　　　　　(C)9:30.　　　　　　(D)11:50.

　　答案：(B)

9.　W: What do you think of Beijing?（女：你認為北京如何？）

　　M: I stayed in Beijing for a week. I really enjoyed the views there.
　　　（男：我在北京待了一星期。我真的很喜歡那邊的景色。）

　　W: Then you came back home?（女：然後你就回家了？）

　　M: A week is not enough! I spent another six days traveling around.
　　　（男：一星期不夠啦！我另外花了六天四處旅行。）

　　Q: How long did the man spend traveling in Beijing?
　　　（問題：這位男士花了多少時間在北京旅行？）

　　(A)For 13 days.（十三天。）　　　　　　(B)For 2 weeks.（兩星期。）

　　(C)For 6 days.（六天。）　　　　　　(D)For 7 days.（七天。）

　　答案：(A)

10.　W: What is your lucky number, 8 or 6?（女：你的幸運數字是什麼，八或是六？）

　　M: Neither. I like 7. It stands for eating food.
　　　（男：都不是。我喜歡七。它代表著吃東西。）

　　W: My lucky number is 3. It sounds like "rich".

（女：我的幸運數字是三。它聽起來像「有錢」。）

M: Why not choose 8? So many people regard it as their lucky number.

（男：為何不選八？那麼多人把它視為他們的幸運數字。）

W: I don't want to follow.（女：我不想跟潮流。）

Q: What number is the man's lucky number?（問題：這位男士的幸運數字是？）

(A)8.      (B)6.      (C)3.      (D)7.

答案：(D)

11. W: What a nice coat! How much is it?（女：多棒的一件外套啊！它多少錢？）

M: It costs at least 100 yuan.（男：它至少要一百元。）

W: Can I bargain?（女：我可以殺價嗎？）

M: Today is a special day and I can give you 10% discount.

（男：今天是個特別的日子我可以給妳九折優惠。）

Q: How much will the woman pay for the nice coat?

（問題：這位女士將付多少錢買這件好外套？）

(A)10 yuan.      (B)99 yuan.      (C)90 yuan.      (D)100 yuan.

答案：(C)

12. W: How long does it take you to go to school?（女：你上學要花多少時間？）

M: I walk for only five minutes from my home to the underground station. Then the underground takes me 20 minutes to reach Garden Station. I walk up to my school for another ten minutes.（男：從我家到地鐵站只要走五分鐘。然後地鐵花我二十分鐘到花園車站。我走到學校另外要十分鐘。）

W: It seems to be convenient, doesn't it?（女：似乎很便利，不是嗎？）

M: Yes, I am used to it.（男：是的，我習慣了。）

Q: How long does it take the boy from home to school?

（問題：這位男孩要花多少時間從家裡到學校？）

(A)25 min.（二十五分鐘）      (B)35 min.（三十五分鐘）

(C)15 min.（十五分鐘）      (D)20 min.（二十分鐘）

答案：(B)

13. W: Can you tell me your school telephone number as it has moved to a new place?（女：你可以告訴我你們學校的電話號碼嗎因為它搬到新地址了？）

M: Of course. It is 62131009.（男：當然。它是 62131009。）

W: It is the old number, isn't it?（女：這是老的號碼，不是嗎？）

M: I am so sorry. I am confused. The new number should be 61213008.

（男：我真抱歉。我搞混了。新的號碼應該是 61213008。）

Q: What is the new telephone number of the boy's school?

（問題：這位男孩的學校新的電話號碼是？）

(A)61213009.      (B)62131009.      (C)62131008.      (D)61213008.

答案：(D)

14. W: I have put in 2 liters of milk. Then, I have to add 1 liter of water into the milk.（女：我放了兩公升牛奶進去。然後，我必須加一公升水到牛奶裡。）

   M: I'm afraid that will be too much water. The instruction says that 4 liters of milk is mixed with 1 liter of water.

   （男：我恐怕那樣會太多水。說明書說四公升牛奶混合一公升水。）

   W: Let me have a check! Oh, you are right. Thank you!

   （女：讓我撿查一下！。噢，你是對的。謝謝！）

   Q: How much water should the girl add into the 2 liters of milk?

   （問題：這位女孩應該加多少水到兩公升牛奶裡？）

   (A)1 liter.（一公升）　　　　　　　　　(B)2 liters.（兩公升）

   (C)0.5 liter.（零點五公升）　　　　　　(D)0.25 liter.（零點二五公升）

   答案：(C)

15. W: Danny, the lottery number has come out. The numbers are 8, 17, 19, 22, 26, 29 and the lucky number is 32.

   （女：丹尼，樂透號碼開出了。數字是 8, 17, 19, 22, 26, 29 而幸運號碼是 32。）

   M: My lucky number is also 32. That's cool. And the others are 7, 18, 19, 23, 26 and the last is 29.（男：我的幸運號碼也是 32。真酷。其它的數字是 7, 18, 19, 23, 26 而最後一號是 29。）

   W: You got a small prize. Congratulations.（女：你得到一個小獎。恭喜你。）

   Q: How many numbers in the man's ticket are the same as the lottery numbers?

   （問題：這位男士的彩票中有多少個號碼是和樂透號碼相同的？）

   (A)4.　　　　　　(B)5.　　　　　　(C)3.　　　　　　(D)6.

   答案：(A)

16. W: Today is already March 1st. Have you sent the letter to that company?

   （女：今天已經是三月一日。你把那封信寄去那個公司了嗎？）

   M: Of course. I sent it yesterday.（男：當然。我昨天就寄了。）

   W: What was the letter about?（女：那封信是關於什麼的？）

   M: In the letter, I told the company about the several parties during the next year of 2012.（男：在信中，我告訴該公司關於明年 2012 年的幾個派對。）

   Q: What date was it the day before yesterday?（問題：前天的日期是？）

   (A)March 1st.（二三月一日）　　　　　　(B)Feb. 29rd.（二二月二十九日）

   (C)Feb. 28th.（二二月二十八日）　　　　(D)Feb. 27th.（二月二十七日）

   答案：(D)

---

Ⅲ、Listen to the passage and tell whether the following statements are true or false.

（判斷下列句子是否符合你聽到的短文內容,符合用 T 表示,不符合用 F 表示）（7分）

Why is one such a bad number? It is because when the date has this number in it, some bad things always happen. Let me give you some examples. In the midnight of September the twenty-first in Taiwan, the earthquake was very horrible. That night, there were about three thousand people who died in that accident. Many houses collapsed and the mountains moved.

為什麼一是那麼壞的一個數字？因為當日期有這個數字在裡面，總有些壞事發生。讓我給你一些例子。在九月二十一日台灣的午夜，那場地震很恐怖。那個夜晚，有大約三千人在那場意外中死去。很多房屋倒塌還發生走山。

America was attacked by terrorists on September 11 in 2001. The terrorists crashed into America's buildings with airplanes. The terrorists used airplanes to hit many tall buildings in America. There were bombs inside the buildings. When the airplanes hit the tall buildings, the tall buildings and the airplanes exploded. About six thousand people died. How terrible that was! I think the terrorists were crazy. People say that the American emergency number is 911, so the terrorists chose September 11 to attack America. There was a big typhoon on July 11 still in 2001 in Taiwan. Its name was Toraji. Many cities were flooded. Some people died because of landslides. These dates all contain the number "one". I really don't think "one" is a good or lucky number. So we have to be careful on the dates with this number.

美國在 2001 年九月十一日遭到恐怖份子攻擊。恐怖份子以飛機撞入美國的建築物。恐怖份子用飛機攻擊很多美國的高建築物。在建築物內有炸彈。當飛機撞到高建築物時，這高建築物和飛機就爆炸。大約六千人死亡。多麼恐怖啊！我認為恐怖份子們瘋了。人們說美國的緊急求救電話號碼是 911，所以恐怖份子選擇九月十一日攻擊美國。七月十一日同樣是 2001 年，在台灣有個大颱風。它的名字叫桃芝。很多都市都淹水。有些人因為土石流而死。這些日期都包含數字「一」。我真的不認為「一」是個好的或是幸運的數字。所以我們必須在有這個數字的日期小心點。

17. In the writer's opinion, one is an unlucky number.
  （在筆者的看法中，一是個不幸運的數字。）
  答案：(T 對)

18. The earthquake that happened in Taiwan in 2001 killed about 2,000 people.
  （2001年發生在台灣的那場地震造成大約兩千人死亡。）
  答案：(F 錯)

19. The terrorists attacked the U.S. on 9‧11 because they thought one was really a bad number.（恐怖份子在九月十一日攻擊美國是因為他們認為一真的是個壞數字。）
  答案：(F 錯)

20. The airplanes crashed into the tall buildings and luckily flew back to the air base.（飛機撞進了高建築物而後幸運地飛回了航空基地。）
  答案：(F 錯)

21. On 7‧11, a big typhoon attacked Taiwan in 2001.
  （2001年，在七月十一日，一個大颱風襲及了台灣。）
  答案：(T 對)

22. Some people died in the typhoon because the wind took them away.
（有些人在颱風中喪生，因為風把他們吹走了。）

答案：(F 錯)

23. According to the writer, January has the most days on which he will be quite careful.（根據筆者，一月有最多他會頗小心的日子。）

答案：(T 對)

---

**IV、Listen to the passage and fill in the blanks with proper words.（聽短文,用最恰當的詞填空,每格限填一詞）（共7分）**

A serious earthquake hit New Zealand, 30 km west of Christchurch early on Saturday morning. The quake, which had a depth of 20.5 miles, struck around 4:35 a.m. local time and was felt throughout much of the South Island and southern parts of the North Island.

星期六早上稍早，一場嚴重的地震襲及了紐西蘭基督城西方三十公里處。這場地震，深度二十點五英哩，發生於當地時間上午四點三十五分左右，在涵蓋南島大部分地區和北島的南部都可感受到。

Police in Christchurch, New Zealand's second-largest city with a population of about 350,000 people, closed the main business district of the city, with buildings falling into streets, damaging cars and blocking roads.

有大約三十五萬人口的紐西蘭第二大城基督城的警方關閉了市區主要的商業區，有建築物倒在路上，損壞了車輛且阻礙了道路。

The New Zealand government gave the degree as 7.4. The U.S. Geological Survey at first reported it at 7.4 but later changed its figure to 7.1.

紐西蘭政府判定其規模七點四級。美國地質評估機構起初公布它為七點四級，但之後更改它的數值為七點一。

The quake was felt as a long rolling motion lasting up to 40 seconds. The area was continuing to feel aftershocks as strong as degree 4.9.

這場地震感覺像是長的滾動持續長達四十秒。該地區持續感受到強達四點九級的餘震。

New Zealand scientists record around 14,000 earthquakes a year, of which around 20 top degree 5.0.

紐西蘭的科學家一年紀錄到大約一萬四千次地震，其中大約二十次超過五級。

The last serious earthquake was in 1968 when an earthquake measuring 7.1 killed three people on the South Island's West Coast.

上一次的嚴重地震是在 1968 年，一場規模七點一的地震在南島的西岸造成三人死亡。

- A serious earthquake hit New Zealand at around __24__ a.m. local time.
（一場嚴重的地震當地時間上午 4:35 左右襲擊了紐西蘭。）

- Christchurch, New Zealand's second-largest city has a population of about __25__ people.（基督城，紐西蘭第二大都市擁有約三十五萬人口。）

- The U.S. Geological Survey at first reported it at 7.4 but later changed its figure to __26__.
（美國地質評估機構起初公布它為七點四級，但之後更改它的數值為七點一。）

- The quake lasted up to __27__ seconds.（這場地震持續長達四十秒。）

- About __28__ earthquakes happen in New Zealand every year.
（在紐西蘭每年大約發生一萬四千次地震。）

- The last serious earthquake in New Zealand took place in __29__.
（上一次紐西蘭嚴重的地震發生於 1968 年。）

- __30__ people lost their lives in the last serious earthquake.
（三人在上一次的嚴重地震中喪生。）

24. 答案：4:35
25. 答案：350,000
26. 答案：7.1
27. 答案：40
28. 答案：14,000
29. 答案：1968
30. 答案：3

# 夏朵英文

全新英語聽力會考總複習原文及參考答案

# Unit 5

---

Ⅰ、Listen and choose the right picture.（根據你聽到的內容,選出相應的圖片。）（6分）

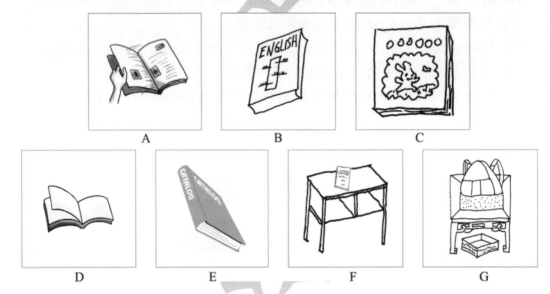

1. The cartoon book is so special that children can draw lovely animals on it.
   （漫畫書是如此地特別,孩子們可以在上面畫可愛的動物。）
   答案：(C)

2. Who laid the book on the desk? Please put it away.
   （是誰把書擱在書桌上?請把它拿開。）
   答案：(F)

3. I can't believe that there are no books inside the bag on that chair.
   （我不能相信在那張椅子上的那個袋子裡沒有書。）
   答案：(G)

4. Class begins. Please turn to page two.（開始上課。請翻到第二頁。）
   答案：(A)

5. It's time to have an English lesson. We should take out our English books.
   （是上英文課的時候了。我們應該拿出我們的英文書。）
   答案：(B)

6. It's a new exercise book and there is enough space where you can take notes.
   （這是一本新的練習本,有足夠的空間讓你可以做筆記。）
   答案：(D)

II、**Listen to the dialogue and choose the best answer to the question.** （根據你聽到的對話和問題，選出最恰當的答案。）（10 分）

7.  M: Have you finished the book?（男：妳看完這本書了嗎？）

    W: I have just finished half of it.（女：我才剛看完一半。）

    M: Oh, my god. You mean you have just read 78 pages?

    （男：噢，我的天。妳的意思是妳才看了七十八頁嗎？）

    W: Yes, but don't worry. I will finish it soon.

    （女：是的，但是別擔心。我很快會看完它。）

    Q: How many pages has the book got?（問題：這本書有多少頁？）

    (A)78 pages.）七十八頁）           (B)80 pages.）八十頁）

    (C)160 pages.）一百六十頁）        (D)156 pages.（一百五十六頁）

    答案：(D)

8.  M: What kind of book do you like best?（男：妳最喜歡哪一類的書？）

    W: I like reading science fiction. What about you?

    （女：我喜歡讀科幻小說。那你呢？）

    M: I prefer cartoons to science fiction. My mother likes love stories.

    （男：比起科幻小說我比較喜歡漫畫書。我母親喜歡愛情故事。）

    W: My mother enjoys only newspapers.（女：我母親只喜歡看報紙。）

    Q: Who enjoys reading cartoons?（問題：誰喜歡讀漫畫書？）

    (A)The girl.）這位女孩）          (B)The boy.）這位男孩）

    (C)The boy's mother.）這位男孩的母親）(D)The girl's mother.（這位女孩的母親）

    答案：(B)

9.  M: What do you think of Harry Porter?（男：妳對哈利波特有什麼看法？）

    W: I have never read a better book than this.（女：我沒有讀過比這更好的書了。）

    Q: What does the woman mean?（問題：這位女士的意思是？）

    (A)This is the best book she has ever read.（這是她所讀過最好的一本書。）

    (B)She doesn't like the book at all.（她一點也不喜歡這本書。）

    (C)She thinks there is a book better than this.（她認為有一本書比這本更好。）

    (D)She doesn't think it is the best book.（她不認為它是最好的書。）

    答案：(A)

10. M: How did you get the book?（男：妳怎麼得到這本書的？）

    W: My father gave it to me as a birthday gift.

    （女：我父親把它當生日禮物送給我的。）

    M: How I wish I could have one!（男：我多希望我能有一本！）

    W: You can borrow it from the library or buy it in the bookstore.

    （女：你可以去圖書館借或者去書店買。）

    M: Why not lend me yours?（男：為什麼不把妳的借我？）

    W: Certainly. Here you are.（女：當然。拿去。）

Q: How will the boy get the book?（問題：這位男孩將如何得到這本書？）
(A)From the library.（從圖書館）　　(B)From the bookstore.（從書店）
(C)From his parents.（從他父母）　　(D)From the girl.（從這位女孩）
答案：(D)

11. M: The book isn't worth reading and isn't attractive, is it?
　　（男：這本書不值得一讀也不吸引人，對不對？）
　　W: No, it isn't.（女：對啊，不值得。）
　　Q: What can we learn from the girl's words?
　　（問題：從這位女孩的說詞我們可以得知？）
　　(A)The girl doesn't enjoy the book.（這位女孩不喜歡這本書。）
　　(B)The girl thinks it is an attractive book.（這位女孩認為這是本吸引人的書。）
　　(C)The girl doesn't know how to answer the question.（這位女孩不知道如何回答
　　　　這問題。）
　　(D)The girl suggests we read the book.（這女孩建議我們讀這本書。）
　　答案：(A)

12. M: Where is my book? I left it on the table just now.
　　（男：我的書在哪裡？我剛剛才把它放在這桌子上。）
　　W: Tomorrow is Monday. So I have put it into your schoolbag on the sofa.
　　（女：明天是星期一。所以我把它放到你在沙發上的書包裡了。）
　　M: Many thanks, Mom.（男：多謝妳，媽媽。）
　　Q: Where is the boy's book?（問題：這位男孩的書在哪裡？）
　　(A)On the sofa.（在沙發上。）　　　(B)On the table.（在桌上。）
　　(C)Under the table.（在桌子下面。）　(D)In his schoolbag.（在他的書包裡。）
　　答案：(D)

13. M: How much is this book?（男：這本書多少錢？）
　　W: The normal price is 76 yuan each. If you buy two, each will be 60 yuan and
　　　　150 for three.（女：正常的價格是每本七十六元。如果你買兩本，每本會是六十
　　　　元，三本一百五。）
　　M: I want to buy two. One is for me and the other for my sister.
　　　　（男：我想買兩本。一本給我而另一本給我姊妹。）
　　W: Let me count how much you have to pay.（女：讓我算算你要付多少錢。）
　　Q: How much will the man pay for the two books?
　　　　（問題：這位男士將付多少錢買這兩本書？）
　　(A)120 yuan.　　　(B)150 yuan.　　　(C)156 yuan.　　　(D)136 yuan.
　　答案：(A)

14. M: What do you often do in your spare time?
　　　　（男：你經常在你的空閒時間做什麼？）
　　W: Seeing films is my favorite. Do you like films?

（女：看電影是我的最愛。你喜歡電影嗎？）

M: I prefer books because books always describe details much better than films.

（男：我比較喜歡書本，因為書總是把細節描述得比電影更好。）

W: In my opinion, films are easy to understand.

（女：依我看來，電影很容易了解。））

Q: Why does the man prefer reading books to watching films?

（問題：為何這位男士和看電影比起來更喜歡讀書？）

(A)Because books are easy to understand.（因為書本很容易了解。）

(B)Because films don't describe details as well as books.

（因為電影不像書把細節描述得那麼好。）

(C)Because films are less interesting than books.（因為電影沒有書那麼有趣。）

(D)Because books are the man's favorite.（因為書本是這位男士的最愛。）

答案：(B)

15. M: Mary, can you lend me this book?（男：瑪莉，妳可以借我這本書嗎？）

W: I'm sorry, Mike. Martin called to borrow it just now.

（女：對不起，麥克。馬丁剛剛才打電話來借它。）

M: That's all right. I can ask for it next week.（男：沒關係。我可以下星期來借它。）

W: But May wanted me to return it this weekend.

（女：但是梅想要我這週末把它歸還。）

Q: Who is the owner of the book?（問題：這本書的主人是誰？）

(A)Martin.（馬丁）    (B)Mike.（麥克）    (C)May.（梅）      (D)Mary.（瑪莉）

答案：(C)

16. M: Look at the picture. The book may be about the school life. But I don't like it as our school life is really boring.（男：看這張圖。這本書可能是關於學校生活。但是我不喜歡它因為我們的學校生活很無趣。）

W: Never judge a book by its cover. Go ahead.

（女：絕對不要以封面判斷一本書。讀吧。）

Q: What can we learn from the woman's words?

（問題：從這位女士的話語中我們可以得知？）

(A)She suggests the boy read the book.（她建議這位男孩讀這本書。）

(B)She agrees with the boy.（她同意這位男孩的說法。）

(C)She doesn't like the cover of the book.（她不喜歡這本書的封面。）

(D)She won't buy the book.（她將不會買這本書。）

答案：(A)

---

Ⅲ、Listen to the passage and tell whether the following statements are true or false.

（判斷下列句子是否符合你聽到的短文內容,符合用 T 表示,不符合用 F 表示）（7分）

Say goodbye to Cindy, the student and say hello to Cindy, the babysitter. That's right — starting in just a few short weeks I am going to be responsible for taking care of a couple of little children for the summer! Can you believe it? I still can't really believe that I actually have a job.

向學生辛蒂說再見，向保姆辛蒂說哈囉。對的 - 短短的幾個星期後即將開始了，今夏我將負責照顧一對小孩子！你能相信嗎？我仍然不能真的相信我實際上有個工作。

Just last week, I was sitting in the kitchen when I happened to hear my mom talking to her friend, Mrs. Barb. It sounded like Mrs. Barb was going to put her kids in a day care centre for the summer. I flew out of my seat as fast as I could and started waving my arms in front of my mom's face and finally she asked what I wanted. So I said if Mrs. Barb needed someone to look after her kids, I would love to do it. And guess what? They both thought that was a good idea!

才上星期，我正坐在廚房的時候剛巧聽到我媽媽和她朋友巴布太太在講話。聽起來好像巴布太太今夏將要把她的孩子們寄放在日間托兒中心。我盡快地從我的座位飛出來開始在我媽媽的面前揮舞我的手臂然後終於她問我想要幹嘛。所以我說如果巴布太太需要某個人照顧她的孩子們，我會很樂意來做。然後猜猜怎麼著？她們兩人都認為這是個好點子！

The next day I met the children and they are really great. Adam is three and Samantha is five. Samantha is a bit rude but I think we'll get along just fine. I'm going to start watching them all day on Monday, Wednesday, Thursday and Friday in July and August. Crazy? I've never had a job before. I hope I will be able to handle it.

次日我和孩子們見面，他們真的好棒。亞當三歲而珊曼莎五歲。珊曼莎有點粗魯但是我認為我們將會好好相處。七月和八月的星期一、星期三、星期四和星期五，我將開始全天看著他們。很瘋狂吧？我以前從未有過工作。我希望我有能力搞定它。

17. To be a babysitter is the writer's first job. （筆者的第一個工作是當保姆。）
答案：(T 對)

18. Cindy is the name of one of the babies the writer is going to take care of.
（辛蒂是筆者將要去照顧的嬰兒其中一人的名字。）
答案：(F 錯)

19. When the writer's mom was talking with her friend last week, the writer was sitting in her bedroom.
（上星期當筆者的媽媽正在和她的朋友講話時，筆者正坐在她房間裡。）
答案：(F 錯)

20. When the writer was waving her arms to her mom, her mom understood what the writer meant.

（當筆者正在向她媽媽揮舞手臂時，她媽媽明白筆者的意思。）

答案：（F 錯）

21. Mrs. Barb was a little bit worried about the writer, but the writer never gave up.（巴布太太有點擔心筆者，但是筆者從未放棄。）

答案：（F 錯）

22. The writer is going to do the job four times a week.

（筆者將一星期做這個工作四次。）

答案：（T 對）

23. The writer has little confidence in getting on well with the babies.

（筆者對和嬰兒們好好相處有很少的信心。）

答案：（F 錯）

---

**IV、Listen to the passage and fill in the blanks with proper words.**（聽短文,用最恰當的詞填空,每格限填一詞）（共 7 分）

If you want to have a great lunch, follow these five rules:

如果你想要一頓很棒的午餐，遵照這五個規則：

One: Choose fruits and vegetables. They make your plate more colorful and they're packed with vitamins and fiber. It's a good idea to eat five kinds of fruits and vegetables every day, so try to fit in one or two at lunch.

一：選擇水果和蔬菜。它們讓你的盤子更色彩豐富且它們充滿了維他命和纖維。每天吃五種水果和蔬菜是個好主意，所以盡量在午餐吃上一兩種。

Two: Know the facts about fat. Kids need some fat in their diets to stay healthy — it also helps keep you feeling full — although you don't want to eat too much of it. Some higher-fat lunch foods include hot dogs and cheese. Don't worry if you like these foods! But you may want to eat them less often and in smaller portions.

二：知道關於脂肪的真相。孩子們的飲食中需要一些脂肪以維持健康 - 它也幫助讓你感到飽足 - 雖然你不想要吃太多。有些高脂肪午餐食物包括熱狗和起司。如果你喜歡這些食物也別擔心！但是你也可能會想不要那麼常吃且吃較小份量的。

Three: It's not just about what you eat, drinks are also good choices, too! Milk has been a favorite lunchtime drink for a long time. If you don't like milk, choose water.

三：它不只是關於你吃什麼，飲料也是好的選擇！牛奶長期以來一直是午餐時間最受喜愛的飲料。如果你不喜歡牛奶，選擇水。

Four: Balance your lunch. When people talk about balanced meals, they mean the meals that include a mix of food groups: some grains, some fruits, some vegetables, some meat or protein foods, and some dairy foods such as milk and cheese. Try to do this with your lunch. A double order of hot dogs, for example, would not make for a balanced lunch.

四：平衡你的午餐。當人們談論到平衡餐食，他們是指一餐包含了混合的食物種類：一些穀類、一些水果、一些蔬菜、一些肉或蛋白質食物，還有一些奶類食物像是牛奶和起司。試著在你的午餐這樣做。例如雙份熱狗就不是一頓平衡的午餐。

Five: Mix it up. Do you eat the same lunch every day? If that lunch is a hot dog, it's time to change your routine. Eating lots of different kinds of foods gives your body a variety of nutrients.

五：把它混合起來。你每天吃相同的午餐嗎？如果那個午餐是熱狗，那是改變你習慣的時候了。吃很多不同種類的食物給你的身體多種類的營養。

- Please __24__ the five steps if you want to have a great lunch.
  （請遵照這五個步驟如果你想要有一頓很棒的午餐。）
- One: Choose fruits and vegetables which can make your __25__ colorful.
  （一：選擇可以讓你的盤子色彩豐富的水果和蔬菜。）
- Two: Know the facts about fat. Eat less often and in __26__ portions.
  （二：知道關於脂肪的真相。不要常吃且吃較小份量。）
- Three: Drinks are also good __27__.（三：飲料也是好的選擇。）
- Four: Balance your lunch and a __28__ order of hot dogs isn't a balanced one.
  （四：平衡你的午餐，雙份熱狗不是平衡的一餐。）
- Five: __29__ the lunch up. Eat different kinds of food.
  （五：把午餐混合起來。吃不同種類的食物。）
- Different foods provide a __30__ of nutrients.
  （不同的食物提供多種類的營養。）

24. 答案：follow（遵照）
25. 答案：plate（盤子）
26. 答案：smaller（較小的）
27. 答案：choices（選擇）
28. 答案：double（雙倍）
29. 答案：Mix（混合）
30. 答案：variety（多種類）

# 夏朵英文

## 全新英語聽力會考總複習原文及參考答案

# Unit 6

I、Listen and choose the right picture.（根據你所聽到的內容,選出相應的圖片。）（6分）

A    B    C

D    E    F    G

1. In the story, Maria lay on the boat in the ocean for a month and finally survived.
   （在這個故事裡，瑪莉亞躺在船上在海上一個月終於生還。）
   答案：(F)

2. The man was surprised to see a pretty girl when he looked at himself in the mirror.（當這位男士照鏡子的時候，他很驚訝看到一位美麗的女孩。）
   答案：(D)

3. This is a special uniform and if you wear it, you will be a powerful guard.
   （這是一件特別的制服，如果你穿上它，你將會變成一位強力的侍衛。）
   答案：(C)

4. Jessica is the queen of the Magic Kingdom. She rules the whole world.
   （潔西卡是魔法王國的女王。她統治這整個世界。）
   答案：(B)

5. Tim has found his flying horse and they have left for the sun.
   （提姆找到了他的飛馬然後他們出發前往太陽。）
   答案：(A)

6. I saw a figure pass in front of my eyes and it looked like a boy.
（我看到一個影子經過我眼前，它看起來像個男孩。）
答案：(E)

II、Listen to the dialogue and choose the best answer to the question. （根據你聽到的對話和問題，選出最恰當的答案。）(10分)

7. W: Are you interested in the science fiction? （女：你對科幻小說有興趣嗎？）
   M: I have little interest in it. （男：我對它沒什麼興趣。）
   Q: What does the man mean? （問題：這位男士的意思是？）
   (A)He isn't interested in the science fiction. （他對科幻小說沒有興趣。）
   (B)He is much interested in the science fiction. （他對科幻小說很有興趣。）
   (C)He has a little interest in the science fiction. （他對科幻小說有一點興趣。）
   (D)He likes the book. （他喜歡這本書。）
   答案：(A)

8. W: Danny, yesterday I read a book called We Are on the Mars.
       （女：丹尼，昨天我讀了一本書名字是我們在火星上。）
   M: What do you think of it, Mary? （男：妳認為它如何，瑪莉？）
   W: It is really worth reading. （女：它真的很值得一讀。）
   M: I will take your advice and read it tomorrow.
       （男：我會採納妳的建議明天來讀它。）
   Q: What did Mary do yesterday? （問題：瑪莉昨天做了什麼？）
   (A)She wrote a book. （她寫了一本書。）
   (B)She phoned Danny. （她打電話給丹尼。）
   (C)She talked with Danny. （她跟丹尼講話。）
   (D)She read a book. （她看了一本書。）
   答案：(D)

9. W: Tom, do you know who wrote the book? （女：湯姆，你知道誰寫了這本書嗎？）
   M: It was written by Jerry Smith fifteen years ago.
       （男：這本書是十五年前由傑瑞史密斯所著。）
   W: Really? I was only one year old at that time.（女：真的？我在那時候只有一歲。）
   Q: How old is the girl? （問題：這位女孩多大？）
   (A)50.            (B)14.            (C)16.            (D)51.
   答案：(C)

10. W: I have two tickets for the film Avatar. Will you go with me tomorrow?
       （女：我有兩張電影阿凡達的票。你明天要和我一起去嗎？）
    M: I'm afraid I have to practice playing the piano at home, or my mother will
       never give me pocket money then.
       （男：我恐怕得在家裡練習彈鋼琴，不然我母親將永遠不會給我零用錢了。）

W: I see. I can ask someone else. Take care.
（女：我明白了。我可以去問別人。保重。）

Q: Why won't the boy go to see the film with the girl?
（問題：為什麼這位男孩不會和這位女孩去看電影？）

(A)He has to have piano lessons outside. （他必須在外面上鋼琴課。）

(B)He has to take care of her mother. （他必須照顧她的母親。）

(C)He has no pocket money. （他沒有零用錢。）

(D)He has to listen to his mother. （他必須聽他母親的話。）

答案：(D)

11. W: Where are you going now? （女：你現在要去哪裡？）

M: I am going to pick Jason up at his house and then drive to Zhongshan Park.
There is a book show and we plan to buy some useful materials. （男：我要去傑森家接他然後開車去中山公園。那裏有個書展，我們計畫買些有用的材料。）

W: That's cool. Can I go with you? （女：那真酷。我可以和你們去嗎？）

M: Of course. We can meet at the gate of Zhongshan Park.
（男：當然。我們可以在中山公園大門口碰面。）

Q: What are they going to do? （問題：他們將要做什麼？）

(A)To buy books. （去買書。）

(B)To pick up rubbish. （去撿垃圾。）

(C)To play in Zhongshan Park. （去中山公園裡玩。）

(D)To visit Jason. （去拜訪傑森。）

答案：(A)

12. W: Jack. It's already 10:50. You should go to bed.
（女：傑克。已經十點五十分了。你應該上床睡覺。）

M: Mom, can I have another twenty minutes? I want to finish the book.
（男：媽，我可以再耽誤二十分鐘嗎？我想看完這本書。）

W: Go ahead. But please remember to protect your eyes.
（女：好吧。但是請記得保護你的眼睛。）

Q: When will Jack go to bed? （問題：傑克將在幾點上床睡覺？）

(A)10:30.　　　　(B)11:10.　　　　(C)10:50.　　　　(D)11:35.

答案：(B)

13. W: Roy, who will attend today's parent meeting for you?
（女：羅伊，誰會為你來參加今天的母姊會？）

M: My uncle will come today. （男：我叔叔今天會來。）

W: What about your parents? （女：那你的父母呢？）

M: My father is on business in Beijing and my mother has to take care of my
sick grandmother. （男：我父親在北京出差而我母親必須照顧我生病的祖母。）

Q: What will Roy's uncle do from the dialogue?
（問題：根據這段對話羅伊的叔叔將要做什麼？）

(A)He will meet Roy at school.（他將會到學校和羅伊會面。）

(B)He will take care of the sick grandmother.（他將會照顧生病的祖母。）

(C)He will go to Beijing for business.（他將會去北京出差。）

(D)He will attend the parent meeting.（他將會參加母姊會。）

答案：(D)

14. W: Hello, this is Doctor Wang's office. Can I help?

（女：哈囉，這裡是王醫師的辦公室。我能效勞嗎？）

M: This is Ben speaking. I wonder if I can meet Doctor Wang at 10 tomorrow morning.（男：我是班。我想知道我能不能明天早上十點鐘和王醫師會面。）

W: Let me check. He won't finish his first operation until 10:30. I think 11 o'clock will be a right time.（女：讓我查一查。他的第一檔手術在十點三十分之前不會結束。我想十一點會是個適合的時間。）

M: OK, let's make it. See you tomorrow.（男：好的，就這麼說定了。明天見。）

Q: When will Ben meet Doctor Wang tomorrow?

（問題：班明天幾點會和王醫師會面？）

(A)At ten o'clock.（十點）　　　　　　(B)At ten thirty.（十點半）

(C)At eleven o'clock.（十一點）　　　　(D)At eleven thirty.（十一點半）

答案：(C)

15. W: Would you like something to drink, coffee or tea?

（女：您想要喝點什麼嗎，咖啡或是茶？）

M: Coffee, please.（男：咖啡，麻煩您。）

W: But there is no milk left.（女：但是沒有牛奶了。）

M: No problem. I enjoy black coffee.（男：沒問題。我喜歡黑咖啡。）

Q: What does the man want to drink?（問題：這位男士想要喝什麼？）

(A)Black tea.（黑茶）　　　　　　　　(B)Black coffee.（黑咖啡）

(C)Milk tea.（奶茶）　　　　　　　　(D)Coffee with milk.（咖啡加奶）

答案：(B)

16. W: Nick, I am reading an English book. But I have met with many new words. What can I do then?

（女：尼克，我正在讀一本英文書。但是我遇到很多生字。那我怎麼辦？）

M: Don't worry. Actually, you can deal with these new words in many ways.

（男：別擔心。實際上，妳能夠以很多方法處理這些生字。）

W: I think I have to record the new words and look them up in the dictionary.

（女：我想我必須記錄這些生字然後在字典裡面查它們。）

M: It is one of the ways. But while reading, you'd better guess the meanings from the context.

（男：這是一個方法。但是在閱讀中，妳最好從內文猜測它的意義。）

Q: What does Nick suggest the lady do to deal with new words while reading?

（問題：尼克建議這位淑女如何在閱讀中處理生字？）

(A)Guess meanings.（猜測其意義。） (B)Use dictionaries.（用字典。）
(C)Take notes.（做筆記。） (D)Record problems.（記錄問題。）

答案：(A)

---

**Ⅲ、Listen to the passage and tell whether the following statements are true or false.**
（判斷下列句子是否符合你聽到的短文內容,符合用 T 表示,不符合用 F 表示）（7 分）

Mr. Jackson worked in a factory. There he drove a truck. He carried the machines that were made in the factory to the station. He drove well so he got more money than his workmates. His wife took good care of him and did all the housework at home.

傑克森先生在一間工廠工作。他在那裡駕駛一台卡車。他載運工廠製造的機器去車站。他駕駛得很好所以他比他的工作同伴們賺更多錢。他的太太把他照顧得很好,在家裡打理所有的家事。

But Mr. Jackson had a shortcoming: he liked drinking. He often drank a little when he had supper. After that he went to bed and soon fell asleep. Mr. Jackson worked still hard so Mrs. Jackson didn't mind.

但是傑克森先生有個短處:他喜歡喝酒。他常常在晚餐時喝一點。那之後他上床去很快就睡著了。傑克森先生仍然努力工作所以傑克森太太並不介意。

One summer afternoon, it was very hot. Mr. Jackson felt tired and thirsty. He stopped by a bar on the side of the road and had a rest. One of his friends saw his truck and asked him to drink. He agreed and they drank a lot. And he didn't wait at the crossing when the lights were red. A policeman tried to stop him, but he drove faster. Soon the policeman found him in the factory and he knew all. He was almost sent away for it. He was very sorry after that and promised he wouldn't drink any more when he was at work.

一個夏天的午後,天氣很熱。傑克森先生感到疲勞且口渴。他停在路邊的一間酒吧前面休息。他的一位朋友看到他的卡車就邀他喝酒。他同意了且他們喝了很多。然後他在十字路口闖了紅燈。一位警察試著阻止他,但是他開得更快。很快地那位警察在工廠找到了他而他也全都知道。為此他幾乎被送走。在那之後他非常懊悔並承諾他工作中將再也不會喝酒。

One day, on his way home, he met an old friend of his. They were both happy and drank much. When he got home, his wife was angry but she didn't say anything and helped him go to bed. The next morning she said, "You drank a lot again last night!" "Who told you about that?" Mr. Jackson called out, "I didn't drink at all!"

一天,在回家的路上,他遇到一位老朋友。他們兩人都很高興且喝了很多。當他回到家,他的太太很生氣但是她沒有說什麼還幫忙把他送上床。第二天早上她說,「你昨晚又喝了很多!」「誰告訴妳的?」傑克森先生叫了出來「我完全都沒喝!」

"But you told me about it yourself!"
但是你自己告訴我的啊！」

"Can you believe what a drinker said?"
妳能相信飲酒者說的話嗎？」

17. Mr. Jackson's job was to move machines into his factory.
（傑克森先生的工作是把機器搬進他的工廠。）
答案：(F 錯)

18. Mr. Jackson could earn more money because he was good at driving.
（傑克森先生可以賺比較多錢因為他很擅長駕駛。）
答案：(T 對)

19. Mr. Jackson often drank wine after supper.
（傑克森先生常常在晚餐後喝葡萄酒。）
答案：(F 錯)

20. Mr. Jackson agreed to drink with his friend and drank a little.
（傑克森先生同意和他的朋友一起喝酒而喝了一點。）
答案：(F 錯)

21. Mr. Jackson didn't stop with the red light on and was caught by the police at the crossing.（傑克森先生沒有在紅燈停下來而被警察在十字路口抓到。）
答案：(F 錯)

22. When Mr. Jackson drank again, his wife got angry and argued with him seriously.（當傑克森先生再次飲酒，他的太太生氣了並且和他嚴重地爭吵。）
答案：(F 錯)

23. The next morning, when Mrs. Jackson told her husband that he drank much, Mr. Jackson didn't want to admit.
（第二天早上，當傑克森太太告訴她先生說他喝很多，傑克森先生不想承認。）
答案：(T 對)

**IV、Listen to the passage and fill in the blanks with proper words.**（聽短文,用最恰當的詞填空,每格限填一詞）（共 7 分）

A Chinese mountain has been renamed in honor of the film Avatar.
一座中國的山為了紀念電影阿凡達而被重新命名。

The Southern Sky Column in Zhangjiajie, Hunan Province, will now be known as the Avatar Mountain. Local officials said photographs of the mountain had been used as the basis for Avatar's fictional world of Pandora.

湖南省張家界的南天一柱，現在將被認定為阿凡達山。當地官員說這座山的照片被用來當作阿凡達的虛構世界潘朵拉的藍圖。

Avatar has become the most popular film ever in China, making $ 80 million at the box office so far. It is said that a photographer from Hollywood had visited the Wulingyuan Scenic Area, the location of the mountain. Many pictures he took then become examples for various elements in the Avatar movie, including the mountains.

阿凡達已成為中國歷年來最受歡迎的電影，目前為止創造了八千萬票房。據說好萊塢的一位攝影師造訪了武陵源自然風景區，此山的所在地。很多他所拍的照片後來成為阿凡達電影中各種元素的範例，包括這些山。

The renaming of the mountain is one of the several attempts made by Zhangjiajie to attract more tourists on the success of Avatar. The government website has also used the slogan "Pandora is far but Zhangjiajie is near".

這座山的重新命名是要使張家界藉著阿凡達的成功吸引更多觀光客的數個企劃之一。政府的網站也使用了「潘朵拉很遠但是張家界很近」的口號。

The film has been showing on 2,500 screens across China. It is a great success.

這部電影在中國各地兩千五百個電影院上映。它是個偉大的成功。

- The __24__ Sky Column in Zhangjiajie will now be known as the Avatar Mountain.
  （張家界的南天一柱現在將被認定為阿凡達山。）
- The mountain had been used as the basis for Avatar's __25__ world of Pandora.（此山被用來當作阿凡達虛構世界潘朵拉的藍圖。）
- Avatar has become the most __26__ film in China.
  （阿凡達已成為中國最受歡迎的電影。）
- A Hollywood photographer's __27__ helped create the world of Avatar.
  （好萊塢的一位攝影師的照片幫助創造了阿凡達的世界。）
- Zhangjiajie __28__ to attract more tourists by renaming the mountains.
  （張家界企圖透過此山的重新命名吸引更多觀光客。）
- The government website has used the slogan "Pandora is __29__ but Zhangjiajie is near".
  （政府網站使用了「潘朵拉很遠但是張家界很近」的口號。）
- The film Avatar has been showing on __30__ screens throughout China.
  （電影阿凡達在中國各地兩千五百個銀幕上映。）

24. 答案：Southern（南方的）
25. 答案：fictional（虛構）
26. 答案：popular（受歡迎）
27. 答案：pictures（照片）
28. 答案：attempts／tries（企圖）
29. 答案：far（遠）
30. 答案：2,500

# 夏朵英文

# Unit 7

---

Ⅰ、Listen and choose the right picture.（根據你聽到的內容,選出相應的圖片。）（6分）

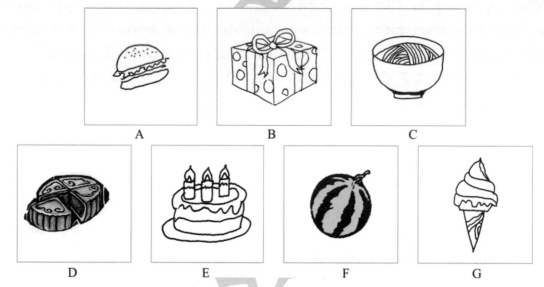

A           B           C

D        E        F        G

1.  My brother's favourite food is ice cream.（我兄弟最喜歡的食物是冰淇淋。）
    答案：(G)

2.  Christmas is always what children can't wait as they can receive presents.
    （孩子們總是等不及聖誕節因為他們可以收到禮物。）
    答案：(B)

3.  Mid-autumn is coming and it's time to taste moon cakes.
    （中秋節要到了，是品嚐月餅的時候了。）
    答案：(D)

4.  Eating noodles on birthday stands for a longer and healthier life.
    （在生日那天吃麵象徵著更長和更健康的人生。）
    答案：(C)

5.  My favorite fast food restaurant is Burger King. I can find the best hamburgers
    there.（我最喜歡的速食餐廳是漢堡堡王。我可以在那裡找到最好的漢堡。）
    答案：(A)

6.  We can also eat water melons in winter but at a higher price.
    （我們也可以在冬天吃到西瓜但是價錢比較貴。）
    答案：(F)

7. M: What would you like for breakfast?（男：妳早餐想吃什麼？）

   W: I want some eggs and bread. A cup of milk will be nice too.

    （女：我想要一些蛋和麵包。一杯牛奶也會很好。）

   M: Would you like some bacon?（男：妳想要一些培根嗎？）

   W: No, thanks.（女：不，謝了。）

   Q: What doesn't the woman want for breakfast?

    （問題：這位女士早餐不想吃什麼？）

   (A)Milk.（牛奶）    (B)Eggs.（蛋）    (C)Bacon.（培根）    (D)Bread.（麵包）

   答案：(C)

8. M: When is your mother's birthday?（男：妳母親的生日是哪時候？）

   W: It was yesterday, November 3rd.（女：是昨天，十一月三日。）

   M: Really? I should have prepared a gift.（男：真的嗎？我應該準備個禮物的。）

   Q: What's the date today?（問題：今天的日期是？）

   (A)Nov. 2nd.（十一月二日）    (B)Oct. 31st.（十月三十一日）

   (C)Nov. 3rd.（十一月三日）    (D)Nov. 4th.（十一月四日

   答案：(D)

9. M: I will go to Hong Kong to spend my holiday.（男：我將去香港度假。）

   W: That's cool. Will you go alone or with someone else?

    （女：那真酷。你會獨自去還是和別人一起去？）

   M: One of my colleagues will go with me as it is organized by my company.

    （男：我的一位同事將和我一起去因為這是我的公司安排的。）

   Q: Who will go with the man?（問題：誰將會和這位男士一起去？）

   (A)His workmate.（他的工作夥伴。）    (B)His classmate.（他的同班同學。）

   (C)His deskmate.（他的同桌夥伴。）    (D)His roommate.（他的室友。）

   答案：(A)

10. M: Hurry up. Mom is waiting for us at the gate.（男：快點。媽媽在大門口等我們。）

   W: But I have to hand in the assignment to Mrs. Wang. She wants to check it

    face to face.（女：但是我必須把這個作業繳交給王太太。她想要當面檢查它。）

   M: Anyway. Be quick.（男：無論如何。快點。）

   Q: Where does this dialogue take place?（問題：這段對話在哪裡發生？）

   (A)At the cinema.（在電影院。）    (B)In the hospital.（在醫院。）

   (C)At a library.（在圖書館。）    (D)At school.（在學校。）

   答案：(D)

11. M: Can we meet at 3 in the afternoon?（男：我們可以在下午三點碰面嗎？）

   W: I think 3:30 may be fine as I have to give a report to my boss.

    （女：我想三點半好了，因為我必須交一份報告給我老闆。）

M: OK. And I give you 30 more minutes. That will be enough for you to give a wonderful report.

（男：好。我多給你三十分鐘。那將會足夠讓你交一份很讚的報告。）

W: You are so nice. See you soon.（女：你人真好。待會見。）

Q: When will they meet?（問題：他們將幾點碰面？）

(A)At 4 o'clock.（四點）        (B)At 3:30.（三點半）

(C)At 3 o'clock.（三點）        (D)At 2:30.（兩點半）

答案：(A)

12. M: Have you read the book I gave you yesterday?

（男：妳讀了我昨天給妳的那本書嗎？）

W: Yes. I always listen to you.（女：是啊。我總是聽你的話。）

M: How do you like it?（男：你認為它如何？）

W: To be frank, it is the last book that I want to read.

（女：坦白說，那是我最不想讀的一本書。）

Q: What does the girl think of the book?（問題：這位女孩認為這本書如何？）

(A)Exciting.（精彩）        (B)Meaningful.（有意義）

(C)Terrible.（糟糕）        (D)Interesting.（有趣）

答案：(C)

13. M: Who is the lady over there?（男：在那邊的那位女士是誰？）

W: She is my aunt, a famous doctor in our town.

（女：她是我阿姨，我們鎮上一位著名的醫師。）

M: Then I know why I feel so familiar. Is her husband a policeman?

（男：那我知道為什麼我看她那麼面熟了。她的丈夫是位警察嗎？）

W: Yes. How do you know that?（女：對。你怎麼知道的？）

M: He works with my father.（男：他和我父親一起工作。）

Q: What is the boy's father's job?（問題：這位男孩的父親的工作是？）

(A)A doctor.（一位醫師。）        (B)A policeman.（一位警察。）

(C)A teacher.（一位教師。）        (D)A worker.（一位工人。）

答案：(B)

14. M: Would you mind my smoking here?（男：妳介意我在這裡抽菸嗎？）

W: I'm afraid you can't smoke here as my kid has had a sore throat.

（女：我恐怕妳不能在這裡抽菸因為我的小孩喉嚨痛。）

M: I'm so sorry and I will listen to you.（男：真抱歉，我會聽妳的話。）

Q: What happened to the lady's child?（問題：這位淑女的孩子怎麼了？）

(A)He smoked a lot.（他抽很多煙。）

(B)He began to smoke.（他開始抽菸。）

(C)He had a sore throat.（他喉嚨痛。）

(D)He threw the cigarettes away.（他把香菸丟掉。）

答案：(C)

15. M: I have ordered fried chicken and the rice with daily soup. What else do you want?（男：我點了炸雞和米飯配例湯。妳還想要什麼別的？）

W: Let me see. Oh, the pictures in the menu always make me confused.
（女：我看看。噢，菜單上的圖片總是讓我很迷惑。）

Q: Where are they now?（問題：他們現在在哪裡？）

(A)In a restaurant.（在一間餐廳裡。）　　(B)At school.（在學校。）

(C)In the kitchen.（在廚房裡。）　　(D)In a flower market.（在花卉市場。）

答案：(A)

16. M: Mrs. Lee, what have you learnt this term?
（男：李太太，妳這學期學到了什麼？）

W: I have learnt how to operate computers and how the piano is played.
（女：我學到了如何操作電腦和鋼琴是怎麼彈的。）

M: What else have you learnt?（男：另外妳還學到什麼？）

W: I have learnt taking good pictures this year and please support me.
（女：我今年學到如何拍好的照片，請支持我。）

M: Of course! But we wonder how you can do that.
（男：當然！但是我們不知道妳如何可以做到。）

W: Please remember, never too old to learn.（女：請記住，學習永遠不嫌老。）

Q: What can we learn from the woman's words?
（問題：從這位女士的話語中我們可以得知？）

(A)She is too old and she wants to give up learning more.
（她太老了她想放棄學更多。）

(B)She thinks it is wise to learn at one's early age.
（她認為在一個人年輕時學習是明智的。）

(C)She won't stop learning till her death.（她一直到死都不會停止學習。）

(D)She is afraid of learning too much as it wastes time.
（她害怕學習太多因為這會浪費時間。）

答案：(C)

---

**Ⅲ Listen to the passage and tell whether the following statements are true or false.**
（判斷下列句子是否符合你聽到的短文內容,符合用 T 表示,不符合用 F 表示）（7分）

Jim, who was twenty-one years old, got a job in a big factory in another town. He left home and found a comfortable flat. He lived there on his own.

吉姆，二十一歲，在另一個城鎮的大工廠裡得到一個工作。他離開家找到一間舒適的公寓。他獨自住在那裏。

At first he cleaned it himself, but he did not want to tire himself out, so he decided to find someone to do the housework. He asked a lot of his fellow workers at the factory what they did about this, and one of the men said, "Oh, Mrs. Roper cleans my flat. She washes the dishes, irons my shirts, keeps the place neat and tidy and so on. I'll introduce her to you if you like. She's a charming old lady." So the next evening Mrs. Roper came to see Jim, and she agreed with pleasure to come to his flat every morning and work for an hour.

起初他自己打掃，但他不想讓自己累壞，所以他決定找個人來做家事。他問了很多他在工廠的工作夥伴他們都怎麼處理，其中一位男士說，「喔，羅培太太打掃我的公寓。她洗碗盤，熨燙我的襯衫，維持環境整潔和之類的。如果你有興趣我會把她介紹給你。她是一位迷人的老婦人。」所以次日的晚上羅培太太來看吉姆，她欣然答應每天早上到他的公寓工作一小時。

After she worked for Jim for two weeks, he looked at the mirror in his bedroom and thought, "That mirror looks very dusty. Mrs. Roper must have forgotten to clean it." He wrote a message in the dust with his finger, "I'm coughing whenever I breathe because the mirror in this room is very dusty."

她為吉姆工作了兩星期之後，他看著他臥室的鏡子想到，「那面鏡子看起來很多灰塵。羅培太太一定是忘記擦它了。」他用他的手指在灰塵上留言道，「每當我呼吸我都咳嗽，因為這房間裡的鏡子有很多灰塵。」

He came home at seven o'clock that evening. Having eaten his supper, he went into his bedroom and looked at the mirror. "That silly woman still hasn't cleaned it!" he said to himself. "All it needs is a cloth!"

他那天晚上七點中回到家。吃了他的晚餐，他去他的臥室且看著那面鏡子。「那位笨女人仍然沒有擦它！」他對他自己說。「它所需要的只是一塊布！」

But then he bent down and in front of the mirror he saw a bottle which he had never seen. He picked it up and found some words on it. He read the words, "Cough medicine".

但是當他在鏡子前彎下腰來他看到一個從未見過的瓶子。他把它拿起來發現上面有些字。他讀了這些字，「咳嗽藥。」

17. Jim lived alone in another town as he worked there.
（吉姆在另一個城鎮獨自居住因為他在那邊工作。）
答案：(T 對)

18. Jim didn't like housework and he always made his flat dusty and untidy.
（吉姆不喜歡做家事，他總是把他的公寓弄得都是灰塵且很亂。）
答案：(F 錯)

19. Mrs. Roper was introduced to Jim and came to see Jim the next morning.
（羅培太太被介紹給吉姆，且在第二天早上來看吉姆。）
答案：(F 錯)

20. Jim left a message on a paper to tell Mrs. Roper to clean the mirror.
（吉姆在一張紙上留言叫羅培太太擦那面鏡子。）
答案：(F 錯)

21. Jim was always coughing badly whenever he breathed.
（每當吉姆呼吸，他總是咳嗽得很厲害。）
答案：(F 錯)

22. The cough medicine Mrs. Roper prepared would make Jim deeply moved.
（羅培太太所準備的咳嗽藥會讓吉姆深深感動。）
答案：(F 錯)

23. Mrs. Roper misunderstood Jim's message.（羅培太太誤會了吉姆的留言。）
答案：(T 對)

---

**IV、Listen to the passage and fill in the blanks with proper words.（聽短文,用最恰當的詞填空,每格限填一詞）（共 7 分）**

Having healthy skin tells others that you take good care of yourself. This is very attractive to every type of person. Like the heart and the stomach, skin is a part of your body. It protects you and keeps you from getting sick. How to take care of your skin? — Read on for some tips.

有健康的皮膚就是告訴其他人你把自己照顧得很好。這對每一種人都很有吸引力。像心臟和胃，皮膚是你身體的一部分。它保護你且讓你不會生病。如何照顧你的皮膚？——繼續往下讀一些技巧。

One simple way is to keep your skin clean. Keeping your hands clean is very important because your hands can spread germs to somewhere in your body.

一個簡單的方法是維持你的皮膚清潔。維持你的手乾淨是很重要的，因為你的手可以將細菌散布到你身體的某處。

When washing your hands, you can use warm water and mild soap. You should wash everywhere carefully, such as the palms, the parts between the fingers, and under the nails.

當你洗手時，你可以用溫水和溫和的肥皂。你應仔細地清洗每個地方，像是手心，手指之間，和指甲下面。

When you take a bath, you should use warm water to clean your body. Don't forget to clean the parts under your arms or behind your ears! Pay attention to your face, especially when you are young. It's a good idea to wash your face once or twice daily with warm water.

當你泡澡，你應用溫水清潔你的身體。別忘了清潔你腋下的部分或耳朵背後！留意你的臉，特別是當你年輕的時候。每天用溫水洗臉一兩次是個好主意。

Besides, drink enough water. Water can make your skin softer and brighter.
另外，喝足夠的水。水可以讓你的皮膚更柔軟且更明亮。

Taking good care of your skin today will keep you away from future problems.

- Healthy skin is __24__ to all kinds of people.
  （健康的肌膚對每一種人都很有吸引力。）
- Keeping your hands clean can stop germs from being __25__ to other places.
  （維持你的手清潔可以阻止細菌散布到其他地方。）
- We'd better use warm water and mild __26__ to wash hands.
  （我們最好用溫水和溫和的肥皂洗手。）
- Remember to clean the __27__ under your arms or behind your ears during a bath. （在泡澡時記得要清潔你腋下的部分或你耳朵背後。）
- It is wise to wash your face once or twice __28__ with warm water.
  （每天用溫水洗一兩次臉是明智的。）
- Drinking enough water makes your skin brighter and __29__.
  （喝足夠的水讓你的皮膚更明亮且更柔軟。）
- You will have fewer __30__ problems if you take good care of your skin.
  （你會有較少未來的問題如果你好好照顧你的皮膚。）

24. 答案：attractive（吸引力）
25. 答案：spread（散布）
26. 答案：soap（肥皂）
27. 答案：parts（部分）
28. 答案：daily（每日）
29. 答案：softer（更柔軟）
30. 答案：future（未來）

# 夏朵英文

## 全新英語聽力會考總複習原文及參考答案

# Unit 8

I、Listen and choose the right picture.（根據你聽到的內容,選出相應的圖片。）（6分）

1. In summer, we can see frogs making special sound on big leaves around the pond.（在夏天，我們可以看到青蛙在池塘四周的大葉子上發出特殊的聲音。）

   答案：(F)

2. How happily the lovely koala is playing on the tree!

   （可愛的無尾熊在樹上玩得多麼快樂啊！）

   答案：(A)

3. A big tree provides shelter and even food for animals and human beings.

   （一棵大樹提供遮避甚至食物給動物和人類。）

   答案：(E)

4. Two swallows are flying across the trees and flowers. It's time for spring.

   （兩隻燕子在樹林和花朵中飛來飛去。是春天的時節了。）

   答案：(B)

5. Sometimes we can find wild pigs in the bush and they are fierce.

   （有時候我們可以發現野豬在灌木叢中，他們很兇猛。）

   答案：(G)

6. Lions are called the king of animals. They have strength and power.

   （獅子被稱為動物之王。他們強而有力。）

答案：(D)

7.　W: What do you plan to do on Tree-planting Day? （女：你在植樹節打算做什麼？）

　　M: We decide to plant some trees around the picnic area in the Century Park.
　　　（男：我們決定在世紀公園中的野餐區四周栽種一些樹木。）

　　W: The Century Park? There are a lot of items for amusement and we can even boat on the river.
　　　（女：世紀公園？那邊有很多娛樂設施，我們甚至可以在河上划船。）

　　M: But we have to wait for the next time. （男：但我們得等下次了。）

　　Q: What are they going to do in the Century Park?
　　　（問題：他們打算在世紀公園裡做什麼？）

　　(A)Have a picnic. （野餐）　　　　　　　(B)Plant trees. （種樹）
　　(C)Go boating. （划船）　　　　　　　(D)Play for fun. （玩樂）
　　答案：(B)

8.　W: How beautiful the road is! （女：這條路多美啊！）

　　M: Yes. It is said that the staff have planted 25 special trees on either side of the road. （男：是的。聽說工作人員在這路的兩側各栽種了二十五棵特別的樹。）

　　W: It's true. I have counted the trees on the road.
　　　（女：是真的。我數過了這路上的樹。）

　　Q: How many trees are there on both sides of this road?
　　　（問題：在這條路的兩側有多少棵樹？）

　　(A)25.　　　　　　(B)40.　　　　　　(C)70.　　　　　　(D)50.
　　答案：(D)

9.　W: What a coincidence! I met John two days before yesterday.
　　　（女：多麼巧啊！我大前天遇到了約翰。）

　　M: Really? Yesterday I went to church with John as it was Sunday.
　　　（男：真的？昨天因為是星期天我和約翰去了教堂。）

　　Q: When did the woman meet John? （問題：這位女時何時遇到了約翰？）
　　(A)On Thursday. （星期四）　　　　　　(B)On Saturday. （星期六）
　　(C)On Friday. （星期五）　　　　　　　(D)On Monday. （星期一）
　　答案：(C)

10.　W: Tom is good at English and we can get help from him.
　　　（女：湯姆英文很拿手，我們可以找他幫忙。）

　　M: Yes. Tom is also good at Chinese. But I am poor at physics. Who can help me?
　　　（男：是的。湯姆的中文也很拿手。但我的物理很爛。誰可以幫我？）

　　W: Although I am poor at Math, physics is my strength. So I can lend you a hand. （女：雖然我的數學很爛，物理是我的強項。所以我可以幫你。）

Q: Which subject is the girl good at?（問題；這位女孩哪一科強？）

(A)Physics.（物理） (B)Math.（數學）

(C)Chinese.（國文） (D)English.（英文）

答案：(A)

11. W: How is your new flat?（女：你的新公寓如何？）

M: I can enjoy the sunshine for long and my kitchen and bathroom are big too.

（男：我可以長時間享受陽光，而且我的廚房和浴室也很大。）

W: Is life convenient in your neighborhood?（女：你家附近的生活方便嗎？）

M: Sure. The flat is perfect except for the price.

（男：當然方便。這公寓除了價錢都很完美。）

Q: What can we learn from the dialogue?（問題：從這段對話我們可以得知？）

(A)There isn't enough sunshine.（沒有足夠的陽光。）

(B)The kitchen is small.（廚房很小。）

(C)Life there is inconvenient.（那裡的生活不方便。）

(D)The price of the flat is very high.（這公寓的價錢很高。）

答案：(D)

12. W: How do you keep in touch with your mother when at school?

（女：當你在學校時如何和你母親保持聯絡？）

M: Of course by cell phone. I have already recorded the number in my cell phone.（男：當然是用行動電話啊。我已經把電話號碼記錄在我的行動電話裡了。）

W: Can you remember the number?（女：你能記得號碼嗎？）

M: It should be 13617889910...Wait. let me check.

（男：它應該是 13617889910...等等。讓我查一查。）

W: What if you lose your cell phone?（女：如果你遺失了你的行動電話怎麼辦呢？）

M: What you say is reasonable. The right number is 13617789110. I will never forget it.

（男：妳所說的很有道理。正確的號碼是 13617789110。我永遠不會忘記它。）

Q: What is the boy's mother's cell phone number?

（問題：這位男孩的母親的行動電話號碼是？）

(A)13671789110. (B)13617789910. (C)13617789110. (D)13617889910.

答案：(C)

13. W: What would you like to be when you grow up?

（女：當你長大你想要做什麼職業？）

M: I dreamed of being a teacher at the age of ten. But now I have changed my mind as being a teacher is no easy job. I think to be a doctor is a good choice and my parents also want me to do that kind of job.

（男：我十歲的時候夢想做一位教師。但現在我改變了主意因為當教師是個不簡單的工作。我認為當醫師是個好選擇而且我父母也想要我做那類的工作。）

W: I never dream to be a nurse or doctor. I want to be a boss. Hope we can realize our dreams.

（女：我從未夢想做護士或是醫師。我想當老闆。希望我們的夢想可以實現。）

Q: What did the boy want to be in the past?（問題：這位男孩過去想要當什麼？）

(A)A doctor.（一位醫師）　　　　　　　　(B)A teacher.（一位教師）

(C)A nurse.（一位護士）　　　　　　　　(D)A boss.（一位老闆）

答案：(B)

14. W: Danny, would you please go and buy some eggs for me?

（女：丹尼，可以請你去幫我買一些蛋嗎？）

M: Sure. How many eggs do you want, Mom?（男：當然。妳想要多少個蛋，媽媽？）

W: Six is enough. If you want, you can buy an ice-cream.

（女：六個就夠了。如果你想，你可以買一個冰淇淋。）

M: Thanks, Mom. I will be back in ten minutes.

（男：謝謝，媽媽。我十分鐘就回來。）

Q: Where will the boy probably go?（問題：這位男孩大概會去哪裡？）

(A)To a restaurant.（去一間餐廳。）　　　(B)To a dairy.（去一間乳品店。）

(C)To a fridge.（去一個冰箱。）　　　　　(D)To a supermarket.（去一間超市。）

答案：(D)

15. W: Dad, when will Mom be back? I miss her badly.

（女：爸爸，媽媽什麼時候會回來？我非常想念她。）

M: Your mom phoned back ten minutes ago and she said she would be back in one hour.（男：妳媽媽十分鐘前打電話回來，她說她會在一小時後回來。）

W: Minutes seem like years to me now.（女：現在對我來說一分鐘就好像一年。）

M: Don't worry! Come and talk with me, honey.

（男：別擔心！來跟我講講話，甜心。）

Q: How long will the girl wait till her mother returns?

（問題：在她母親回來之前這位女孩將等多久？）

(A)50 min.（五十分鐘）　　　　　　　　(B)60 min.（六十分鐘）

(C)10 min.（十分鐘）　　　　　　　　　(D)70 min.（七十分鐘）

答案：(A)

16. W: Do you like reading newspapers?（女：你喜歡看報紙嗎？）

M: Newspapers can tell us a lot about the world and advertisements also help make our life convenient. However, the letters in newspapers are too small and I can't see them clearly.（男：報紙可以告訴我們很多關於世界的事還有廣告也幫助我們使生活更便利。然而，報紙上的字太小了我看不清楚。）

W: But how do you get the information you need?

（女：那你怎麼得到你需要的資訊？）

M: TV news is my good friend and I can enjoy both sounds and exciting pictures.

（男：電視新聞是我的好朋友，我可以同時享受聲音和精彩畫面。）

Q: Why doesn't the man read newspapers?（問題：為何這位男士不看報紙？）
(A)Because there are many advertisements.（因為有很多廣告。）
(B)Because TV has taken the place of newspapers.（因為電視取代了報紙的地位。）
(C)Because he can hardly see clearly the letters in newspapers.
　　（因為他幾乎不能看清楚報紙上的字。）
(D)Because he likes moving pictures.（因為他喜歡動態畫面。）
答案：(C)

---

Ⅲ、Listen to the passage and tell whether the following statements are true or false.
（判斷下列句子是否符合你聽到的短文內容,符合用 T 表示,不符合用 F 表示）(7分)

Work today is very different from the way it was fifty or even twenty years ago. In the past, most people got up early in the morning, traveled to their factories by bus, train or car, worked eight hours and traveled home again.

今天的工作方式和五十年甚至二十年前有很大的不同。在過去，大多數人早上早起，搭巴士、火車或汽車到他們的工廠，工作八小時然後再次通勤回家。

In today's world, many companies are changing this type of working. More and more people work from home. This means that they needn't travel to an office every day. This is possible, of course, because of technology like the Internet, the fax and video telephones where you can see other people when you talk to each other. These telephones also let you talk to many people at the same time. The money is the same, but there is less time wasted on communication.

在今天的世界，很多公司改變了這種工作形式。愈來愈多人在家工作。這意味著他們不需要每天通勤到辦公室。當然，這是可能的，這是由於網際網路、傳真和當你說話時可以看到彼此的視訊電話的科技。這種電話也讓你同時和很多人一起講話。價錢是相同的，但是浪費在交通上的時間較少。

Is it better or worse than working in an office? Well, if you work from home and your neighbor doesn't, you're getting up when he is leaving for the office at 7:00. He is sitting in his car at 7:30, and you're drinking a cup of coffee and checking your emails. At 8:00, when your neighbor is arriving at the office, you're taking a shower. After that, you have breakfast and begin your day's work. You send several reports by email, and then you have a meeting over the video telephone with your customers in Brazil and Italy. At lunchtime you aren't very hungry, so you decide to continue working. You work until about 4:00, check your emails and then relax. You take your dog to the park for a run. At six o'clock, you're watching the news when your neighbors arrive home.

它比在辦公室工作好還是不好呢？好，如果你在家工作而你的鄰居不是，七點鐘你起床的時候他正要出門去上班。七點半時他正坐在他的車內，而你正在撿查你的電子郵件一邊喝著一杯咖啡。八點鐘，當你的鄰居抵達辦公室，你正在淋浴。那之後，你吃早餐並開始你的一天的工作。你用電子郵件寄幾份報告，然後你在視訊電話上和你在巴西以及義大利的客戶開一個會。午餐時間你沒有很餓,所以你決定繼續工作。你工作到大約四點鐘,撿查你的電子郵件然後放輕鬆。你牽你的狗去公園跑跑。六點鐘,當你正在看電視新聞時你的鄰居回到家。

17. In the past, most people walked to factories quite early.

（在過去,大多數人頗早走路去工廠。）

答案：(F 錯)

18. Only the Internet helps people to work from home.

（只有網際網路幫助人們在家裡工作。）

答案：(F 錯)

19. When neighbors are leaving for their factories, you may be having a bath.

（當鄰居門出門去他們的工廠,你可能正在泡澡。）

答案：(F 錯)

20. Video telephones make it possible talking with more people at the same time.

（視訊電話讓同時和很多人一起說話變得可能。）

答案：(T 對)

21. The pay for the video telephones depends on the number of participants.

（視訊電話的通信費決定於參與的人數。）

答案：(F 錯)

22. You don't need to stop your work if you are not hungry at noon.

（你不需要停下你的工作如果你中午不餓。）

答案：(T 對)

23. Working from home helps save a lot of time that can be spent working and even relaxing.

（在家工作幫助省下很多可以用在工作上和甚至放輕鬆的時間。）

答案：(T 對)

---

IV、Listen to the passage and fill in the blanks with proper words. （聽短文,用最恰當的詞填空,每格限填一詞）（共 7 分）

Earth Hour started in 2007 in Sydney, Australia when 2.2 million homes and businesses turned their lights off for one hour to make their stand against climate change. Only a year later Earth Hour became a global movement with more than 50 million people across 35 countries participating. Global landmarks such as the Sydney Harbor Bridge, the Tower in Toronto, the Golden Gate Bridge in San Francisco, all stood in darkness, as symbols of hope for a cause that grows more urgent by the hour. In March 2009, hundreds of millions of people took part in the third Earth Hour. Over 4,000 cities in 88 countries officially switched off to pledge their support for the planet, making Earth Hour 2009 the world's largest global climate change initiative.

當二百二十萬戶住宅和公司將它們的燈關掉一小時以闡明他們對抗氣候改變的立場，地球一小時 2007 年在澳洲雪梨開始了。才一年之後地球一小時成為全球的運動，有超過五千萬人遍布三十五個國家參與。世界級的地標例如雪梨港灣大橋、在多倫多的加拿大國家塔、舊金山的金門大橋，全都站在黑暗之中，象徵著對每一小時都更加迫切希望的目標。在 2009 年三月，數億人參與了第三次的地球一小時。在八十八個國家超過四千個都市正式熄燈以宣誓他們對地球的支持，使得 2009 年的地球一小時成為全世界最大的地球氣候改變自發運動。

Earth Hour 2010 took place on Saturday, 27 March at 8:30 p.m. and is a global call to action to every individual, every business and every community throughout the world. It is a call to stand up, to take responsibility, to get involved and lead the way towards a sustainable future. Iconic buildings and landmarks from Europe to Asia and the Americas stood in darkness. People across the world from all walks of life turned off their lights and joined together in celebration of the one thing we all have in common for our planet.

2010 年的地球一小時在三月二十七日星期六晚間八點三十分舉行，它是個對全世界各地每一個人每間公司和每個社區的全球行動的呼籲。它是個要大家站起來負起責任一起參與和引領邁向永續未來的呼籲。從歐洲到亞洲和美洲指標性的建築物和地標都站在黑暗中。世界各地過著各種生活的人們關掉了他們的燈一起參加慶祝我們共同擁有的地球。

- Earth Hour started in a country named __24__.
  （地球一小時開始於一個名為澳洲的國家。）
- In 2008, even the Golden Gate __25__ stood in darkness.
  （在 2008 年，連金門大橋都站在黑暗中。）
- In 2009, __26__ countries took part in Earth Hour.
  （在 2009 年，八十八個國家參加了地球一小時。）
- In 2010, Earth Hour was on __27__. The date was March 27th.
  （在 2010 年，地球一小時舉辦於星期六。日期是三月二十七日。）
- Earth Hour 2010 is a call for all human beings to stand up and take __28__.
  （2010 年的地球一小時是對全人類站起來負起責任的呼籲。）
- All famous buildings from __29__ to Asia and the Americas stood in darkness.
  （所有出名的建築物從歐洲到亞洲和美洲都站在黑暗中。）
- We hold Earth Hour just to celebrate the only thing we have in __30__— our planet.
  （我們舉辦地球一小時只是為慶祝我們唯一共同擁有的東西－我們的地球。）

24. 答案：Australia（澳洲）
25. 答案：Bridge（橋）
26. 答案：88
27. 答案：Saturday（星期六）
28. 答案：responsibility（責任）
29. 答案：Europe（歐洲）
30. 答案：common（共同）

# 夏朵英文

## 全新英語聽力會考總複習原文及參考答案

# Unit 9

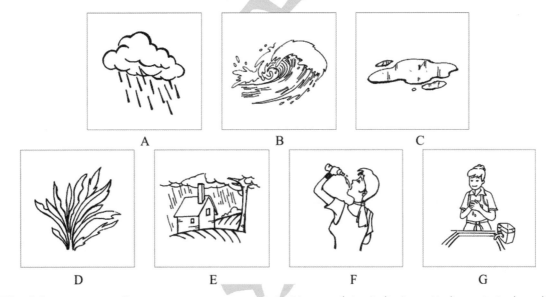

1. The big wave took away many people's lives. （大浪奪走了很多人的生命。）
   答案：(B)

2. This kind of leaves is always seen in rivers and lakes.
   （這種葉子總是可以在河川和湖泊中被看到。）
   答案：(D)

3. When we wash our hands, please don't leave the water running.
   （當我們洗手時,請不要讓水放著流。）
   答案：(G)

4. The heavy rain didn't destroy the well-built house.
   （豪雨沒有摧毀這幢蓋得很好的的房子。）
   答案：(E)

5. It is necessary to drink some water if you finish the exercise.
   （如果你運動完,喝一些水是必要的。）
   答案：(F)

6. I see water on the road. Did it rain just now?
   （我看到路上有水。剛才是不是有下雨?）
   答案：(C)

7.　M: Would you like something to drink, coffee or tea?
　　　（男：您想喝點什麼，咖啡或是茶？）
　　W: Neither. Just some water, please.（女：都不要。只要一些水，麻煩您。）
　　M: OK, wait a minute.（男：好的，等一下。）
　　Q: What would the girl like to drink?（問題：這位女孩想要喝什麼？）
　　(A)Water.（水。）　　　　　　　　　　(B)Coffee.（咖啡。）
　　(C)Tea.（茶。）　　　　　　　　　　　(D)Wine.（葡萄酒。）
　　答案：(A)

8.　M: Have you paid the water bill?（男：妳付了水費帳單嗎？）
　　W: Yes. This month, I used 18 litres of water and each litre costs 6 dollars.
　　　（女：是的。這個月，我用了十八公升的水而每公升要六美元。）
　　M: It is a large sum. Remember to save water.（男：是個大數目。記得要省水。）
　　Q: How much did the lady have to pay for the water she used this month?
　　　（問題：這位淑女為這個月所使用的水需要付多少錢？）
　　(A)18 dollars.（十八美元。）　　　　　(B)80 dollars.（八十美元。）
　　(C)480 dollars.（四百八十美元。）　　(D)108 dollars.（一百零八美元。）
　　答案：(D)

9.　M: How do you save water at school?（男：妳在學校如何省水？）
　　W: I think the best way is to remember to turn off the tap.
　　　（女：我認為最好的方法是記得關掉水龍頭。）
　　M: A lot of students always forget to do so. I think the most important thing is
　　　to help those students to realize the importance of water.（男：一大堆學生總
　　　是忘記這樣做。我認為最重要的事是幫助那些學生們領悟水的重要。）
　　W: I agree with you.（女：我同意你的說法。）
　　Q: What does the man suggest the girl do to save water?
　　　（問題：這位男士建議這位女孩怎樣省水？）
　　(A)Turn off the tap.（關掉水龍頭。）
　　(B)Use less water.（用較少水。）
　　(C)Educate those who waste water.（教育那些浪費水的人。）
　　(D)Tell others to drink less.（叫其他人少喝一點。）
　　答案：(C)

10.　M: My mother is cooking now. Can you stay to have dinner with us?
　　　（男：我母親正在煮飯。妳可以留下來跟我們一起吃晚餐嗎？）
　　W: That's nice. But my father is sick and in bed. I have to go back to cook for
　　　him.（女：真好。但是我父親臥病在床。我必須回去為他煮飯。）
　　M: Can I help?（男：我能幫忙嗎？）

W: I can manage and don't worry about me and my father.
（女：我可以搞定的，別擔心我和我父親。）
Q: What is the girl's father doing now?（問題：這位女孩的父親正在做什麼？）
(A)Seeing the doctor.（看醫生。）　　　　(B)Cooking.（煮飯。）
(C)Having dinner.（吃晚餐。）　　　　　(D)Lying in bed.（躺在床上。）
答案：(D)

11. M: Jane likes watching football and her brother, Jack, enjoys playing basketball.（男：珍喜歡看足球而她兄弟傑克喜歡打籃球。）
W: I know something about them. Their parents are both famous swimmers.
（女：我知道一些關於他們的事。他們的父母都是有名的游泳健將。）
M: Your father is also a well-known tennis player. So do you like it?
（男：妳父親也是位家喻戶曉的網球選手。那麼妳喜歡網球嗎？）
W: I have no interest in it. I just want to learn the best skills of swimming from Jane's mother.（女：我對它沒有興趣。我只想向珍的母親學最好的游泳技巧。）
Q: Which sport is Jack's father good at?（問題：傑克的父親拿手的是哪一項運動？）
(A)Basketball.（籃球）　　　　　(B)Swimming.（游泳）
(C)Tennis.（網球）　　　　　　 (D)Football.（足球）
答案：(B)

12. M: Sally, you are writing a letter on the paper, aren't you?
（男：莎麗，妳在紙上寫一封信，不是嗎？）
W: I have to. My computer has been controlled by my parents for a week.
（女：我必須這樣。我的電腦被我的父母控制一星期了。）
M: I am sorry to hear that. Go ahead.（男：我很遺憾聽到這消息。繼續吧。）
Q: Why doesn't the girl write letters on a computer but on the paper?
（問題：為何這位女孩不在電腦上而在紙上寫信？）
(A)She doesn't want to send an email.（她不想寄電子郵件。）
(B)She has been controlled by the computer.（她被電腦所控制。）
(C)Her parents asked her to write on the paper.（她父母要求她寫在紙上。）
(D)She is not allowed to use the computer.（她不被允許使用電腦。）
答案：(D)

13. M: Where are you from, Maggie?（男：妳從哪裡來的，梅姬？）
W: I lived in the UK when I was young, but I am an American.
（女：我小時候住在英國，但我是美國人。）
M: Why do you choose to work in China?（男：為何妳選擇在中國工作？）
W: The job here is attractive and I want to meet the challenge.
（女：這裡的工作很吸引人而且我想要迎接挑戰。）
Q: Where does the woman work?（問題：這位女士在哪裡工作？）
(A)In the U.K.（在英國。）　　　　(B)In the U.S.A.（在美國。）
(C)In the P.R.C.（在中國。）　　　　(D)In the U.N.（在聯合國。）

答案：(C)

14. M: Have you ever heard about Wolf and Goat?（男：妳可曾聽過「狼和山羊」？）

W: It's about the interesting and funny stories between a lovely goat and a bad wolf.（女：那是關於可愛的山羊和壞狼之間有趣又好笑的故事。）

M: It sounds not bad. What's the duration of it?（男：聽起來不賴。它有多長？）

W: Around two hours.（女：兩小時左右。）

Q: What are they talking about?（問題：他們在談論什麼？）

(A)A movie.（一部電影。） (B)A book.（一本書。）

(C)A magazine.（一本雜誌。） (D)A story.（一則故事。）

答案：(A)

15. M: What's the matter with you, Alice?（男：妳是怎麼了，愛莉絲？）

W: I am not feeling well and have a serious stomachache.

（女：我感覺不太舒服且有嚴重的胃痛。）

M: Did you eat too much or anything spicy this morning?

（男：妳今天早上有吃太飽或任何辣的東西嗎？）

W: In fact, I had nothing for breakfast.（女：實際上，我早餐什麼都沒吃。）

Q: What is probably the reason that the girl has a stomachache?

（問題：這位女孩胃痛可能是什麼原因？）

(A)She ate much spicy food.（她吃太多辣的食物。）

(B)She liked eating too much.（她喜歡吃太多。）

(C)She didn't have her breakfast.（她沒吃早餐。）

(D)She was not feeling well.（她感覺不舒服。）

答案：(C)

16. M: I am sorry I am late for the charity fair, Mrs. Wang.

（男：很抱歉慈善市集我遲到了，王太太。）

W: Better late than never. Come on!（女：遲到總比沒到好。來吧！）

Q: What does the woman mean?（問題：這位女士的意思是？）

(A)She wants the boy never to be late again.（她希望這位男孩再也不要遲到。）

(B)She isn't angry with the boy.（她沒有對這位男孩生氣。）

(C)She wants the boy never to come to the fair.

（她希望這位男孩根本不要來市集。）

(D)She doesn't care about the boy.（她不在乎這位男孩。）

答案：(B)

---

**Ⅲ Listen to the passage and tell whether the following statements are true or false.**

（判斷下列句子是否符合你聽到的短文內容,符合用 T 表示,不符合用 F 表示）(7分)

---

Among national parks, Yellowstone is number one in many ways. It's the first national park in the world and it's the largest park in the United States, with a very large area.

在國家公園當中，黃石公園在很多方面都是第一名。它是全世界第一座國家公園也是美國最大的公園，占地很廣大。

Wild animals in Yellowstone are under good protection. They do not live in cages like animals in most zoos. The park is large enough for animals to walk freely like in the wild. They are able to live in a natural way. Many people have visited the park since it opened in 1872.

黃石公園裡的野生動物都受到很好的保護。牠們不像大多數動物園的動物住在籠子裡。這公園大到足以讓動物自由走動就像在野外。牠們能夠以自然的方式生活。自從它於1872年開放以來很多人參觀過此公園。

Many animals in the park are not afraid of people. Sometimes people can get close to them easily. But people can't hunt or feed animals in the park, because hunting or feeding will disturb animals' life.

此公園裡很多動物不害怕人。有時候人們可以輕易地靠近牠們。但是人們不能在公園內獵捕或餵食動物，因為打獵或餵食會打擾到動物的生活。

Yellowstone National Park sets a good example of how people and wild animals live together peacefully. Putting animals in cages is not a good way to protect them. If people realize the importance of wild animals, they should give animals a comfortable living environment.

黃石國家公園為人類和野生動物如何一起和平生活樹立了一個好的典範。把動物放在籠子裡不是保護牠們的好方法。如果人們了解野生動物的重要性，他們應該給予動物們一個舒適的生活環境。

17. Yellowstone is the first park in America and even in the world.
（黃石公園是美國，甚至是全世界的第一座公園。）
答案：(F 錯)

18. Yellowstone has been open for more than 130 years.
（黃石公園開放已經超過一百三十年。）
答案：(T 對)

19. There are no cages in Yellowstone, but animals are unable to live in a natural way.（在黃石公園裡沒有籠子，但是動物們不能以自然的方式生活。）
答案：(F 錯)

20. Animals in Yellowstone are quite happy if people feed food to them.
（黃石公園裡的動物會頗開心如果人們餵牠們食物。）
答案：(F 錯)

21. Hunting animals in Yellowstone will bring damage to animals' life.
（在黃石公園裡獵捕動物會對動物的生活帶來災害。）
答案：(T 對)

22. People and wild animals live together peacefully in Yellowstone.
（在黃石公園裡人類和野生動物在一起和平地生活。）
答案：(T 對)

23. In most zoos, animals are kept in cages.（在大多數動物園裡，動物被養在籠子裡。）
答案：(T 對)

---

**IV、Listen to the passage and fill in the blanks with proper words.**（聽短文,用最恰當的詞填空,每格限填一詞）（共 7 分）

Rivers are one of our most important natural resources. Many of the world's great cities are located on rivers, and almost every country has at least one river flowing through it that plays an important part in the life of its people.

河川是我們最重要的自然資源之一。世界上很多大都市都位於河川上，幾乎每個國家都有至少一條河川流經，並且在國民的生活中扮演著重要的角色。

Since the beginning of history, people have used rivers for transportation. The longest one in the United States is the Mississippi. The lifeline of Egypt is the Nile, and it is also important for transportation. Ships can travel along it for a thousand miles. Other great rivers are the Congo in Africa and the Mekong in Southeast Asia. The greatest of all for navigation, however, is the Amazon in Brazil. It is so wide and so deep that large ships can go about thousands of miles upon it.

從歷史的開端，人們就利用河川來運輸。美國最長的一條是密西西比河。埃及的生命線是尼羅河，它也因運輸而有其重要性。船隻可以沿著它運行一千英里。其它偉大的河川是非洲的剛果河和東南亞的湄公河。然而，航行上最了不起的是巴西的亞馬遜河。它那麼寬又那麼深所以大船可以在上面航行大約數千英里。

Besides transportation, rivers give food, water to drink, water to irrigate fields, and chances for fun and recreation for the people who live along their banks. However, large cities and industries that are located upon rivers often cause problems. As the cities grow in size and industries increase in number, the water in the rivers becomes polluted with chemicals and other materials. People are realizing the importance of doing more to keep their rivers clean if they want to enjoy the benefits of this natural resource.

運輸之外，河川提供住在它沿岸的人們食物、飲用水、灌溉田園用水和娛樂及休閒的可能性。然而，位於河川上的大都市和工業常常造成問題。隨著都市規模成長和工業數量增加，河川中的水變成被化學藥劑和其他物質所汙染。人們正領悟到多努力維持他們的河川乾淨的重要性，如果他們想要享受這自然資源的好處。

- Rivers, as a kind of __24__ resources, are quite important.
  （河川，因為是一種自然資源，所以頗重要。）
- At least one river __25__ through a country and it plays an important role.
  （至少一條河流經一個國家且它扮演一個重要的角色。）
- The Nile is the longest river worldwide and is the lifeline of __26__.
  （尼羅河是全世界最長的河，且是埃及的生命線。）
- Large ships can go about thousands of miles upon the Amazon because it is so __27__ and wide.
  （大船可在亞馬遜河上航行約數千英里因為它那麼深又寬。）
- Rivers also give food, water to drink, water to irrigate __28__, and chances for fun.（河川也提供食物、飲用水、灌溉田園用水和娛樂的機會。）
- The problem of river pollution is __29__ by chemicals and other materials from large cities or industries located upon rivers.
  （河川污染的問題是來自河川上的大都市或工業的化學藥劑和其他物質所造成。）
- Keeping rivers clean can make human beings enjoy the __30__ of this natural resource.（維持河川乾淨可使人類享受這個自然資源的好處。）

24. 答案：natural 自然
25. 答案：flows 流
26. 答案：Egypt 埃及
27. 答案：deep 深
28. 答案：fields 田園
29. 答案：caused 造成
30. 答案：benefits 好處

# 夏朵英文

全新英語聽力會考總複習原文及參考答案

# Unit 10

I、Listen and choose the right picture. (根據你聽到的內容,選出相應的圖片。)(6分)

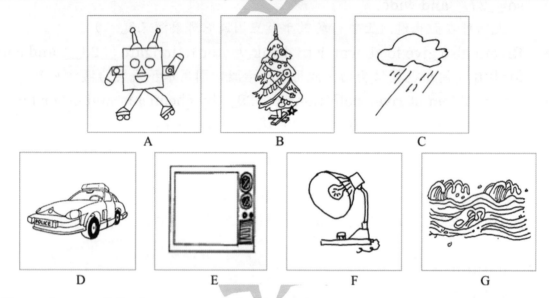

A B C

D E F G

1. Please be careful when you see the lightning. It is quite dangerous.
   （當你看到閃電時請小心。那很危險。）
   答案：(C)

2. With electricity, we can enjoy different programs on TV.
   （有了電,我們可以享受電視上不同的節目。）
   答案：(E)

3. In America, there are some cars which use electricity instead of fuel.
   （在美國,有些汽車用電而非汽油。）
   答案：(D)

4. Don't always keep your light on. It will be a waste of electricity.
   （別老是讓你的燈開著。這樣會浪費電。）
   答案：(F)

5. If we add some small lights to the decorated Christmas tree, it will be perfect.
   （如果我們在裝飾好的聖誕樹上加些小燈,它就會完美了。）
   答案：(B)

6. One of the best ways to make electricity is to make full use of the waves in the oceans. （發電的最好方法之一是完整利用海中的浪。）

答案：(G)

7. M: Why do you hurry to go back?（男：妳為什麼趕著要回去？）
   W: The electric fan is still running. I have to deal with it.
   （女：電風扇仍然開著。我必須去處理它。）
   M: That's a problem. Go ahead.（男：那的確是個問題。去吧。）
   Q: What will the woman do then?（問題：這位女士接著將做什麼？）
   (A)Turn on the fan.（打開電扇。）          (B)Clean the fan.（清洗風扇。）
   (C)Turn off the fan.（關掉風扇。）          (D)Carry the fan.（搬風扇。）
   答案：(C)

8. M: Sally, the radio doesn't work. What's up?（男：莎莉，收音機不能用。怎麼了？）
   W: I will go and buy some new batteries. It will be all right soon.
   （女：我將會去買些新的電池。它很快就能用了。）
   M: Thank you. You are always considerate.（男：謝謝。妳總是很貼心。）
   Q: What's wrong with the radio?（問題：收音機是怎麼了？）
   (A)The quality of the radio is poor.（這收音機的品質很差。）
   (B)There is something wrong with some parts of the radio.
   （這收音機的某些零件有些毛病。）
   (C)The radio is broken.）這收音機壞了。）
   (D)The batteries need changing.（需要更換電池。）
   答案：(D)

9. M: Congratulations. Your new house is wonderful.（男：恭喜。妳的新房子好棒。）
   W: Thank you. We are just moving in.（女：謝謝。我們才剛剛搬進來。）
   M: The electric light is modern. That electric kettle is a new kind. I like the TV
      most. It's so big. The washing machine is big enough to put ten pieces of
      clothing in. The sofa is comfortable and the microwave is really useful.
      （男：電燈好現代感。那個電水壺是新款。我最喜歡電視機。它好大。這洗衣機
      大到夠放十件衣服進去。這沙發很舒適而且這微波爐真的很有用。）
   Q: How many electrical appliances does the man mention in the dialogue?
      （問題：這位男士在對話中提到了多少樣電器設備？）
   (A)Five.（五）      (B)Six.（六）      (C)Four.（四）      (D)Three.（三）
   答案：(A)

10. M: Excuse me, how much is the rice cooker?（男：請問，這個電鍋多少錢？）
    W: It cost 460 yuan last week. But today the price is just half of it.
    （女：它上星期要四百六十元。但是今天價錢只有一半。）
    M: My God. It's so cheap. I will take it.（男：天啊。它好便宜。我要買。）

Q: How much is the rice cooker?（問題：這電鍋多少錢？）
(A)400 yuan.（四百元）　　　　　　(B)460 yuan.（四百六十元）
(C)230 yuan.（二百三十元）　　　　(D)200 yuan.（二百元）
答案：(C)

11. M: The film was shown last Sunday. It was boring.
　　　（男：這部電影上週日播過了。它很無趣。）
　　W: Why not change a channel? You will find more interesting programs.
　　　（女：為何不換台？你會找到比較有趣的節目。）
　　M: That's wise.（男：真睿智。）
　　Q: What are they doing now?（問題：他們現在正在做什麼？）
　　(A)Seeing a film.（看電影。）
　　(B)Watching TV.（看電視。）
　　(C)Swimming across the channel.（游泳橫越海峽。）
　　(D)Discussing the latest film.（討論最新的一部電影。）
　　答案：(B)

12. M: The building used to be beautiful at night. But why is it completely dark?
　　　（男：這棟建築物曾經在晚上很美。但是為什麼它完全黑暗？）
　　W: All the lights are switched off because now the Earth Hour program is being held around the world.
　　　（女：所有燈都被關掉了因為現在地球一小時的活動正在全球舉辦。）
　　M: I thought there was something wrong with the electrical wire.
　　　（男：我還以為是電線有什麼毛病呢。）
　　Q: Why is the building dark?（問題：為何這棟建築物是黑暗的？）
　　(A)Because of something wrong with the wire.（因為電線有毛病。）
　　(B)Because all the lights are broken.（因為所有的燈都壞了。）
　　(C)Because of the bad weather.（因為惡劣的天氣。）
　　(D)Because of a special program.（因為一個特殊的活動。）
　　答案：(D)

13. M: Alice, how long does it take you to cook the dishes for two?
　　　（男：愛莉絲，妳煮兩人份的菜要花多少時間？）
　　W: It depends. If I use the microwave, 20 minutes is enough. If I cook with gas, the time has to be doubled.（女：不一定。如果我用微波爐，二十分鐘就夠了。如果我用瓦斯烹調，時間就需要兩倍。）
　　M: So you prefer to use the microwave?（男：所以妳寧願用微波爐？）
　　W: No, not often.（女：不，我不常用。）
　　Q: How long does it take the woman to cook with gas?
　　　（問題：這位女士用瓦斯烹調要花多少時間？）
　　(A)40 minutes.（四十分鐘。）　　　　(B)20 minutes.（二十分鐘。）
　　(C)Half an hour.（半小時。）　　　　(D)10 minutes.（十分鐘。）

答案：(A)

14. M: Mom, let me help you switch on the light.（男：媽媽，讓我幫妳開燈。）

W: No, never ever. Go and dry your hand.（女：不，千萬不要。去把你的手弄乾。）

M: Yes. I know what I have to do.（男：好的。我知道我必須做什麼。）

Q: Why does the mother not allow the boy to switch on the light?

（問題：為何這位母親不准許這位男孩去開燈？）

(A)He doesn't know how to do it.（他不知道怎麼做。）

(B)He should wash his hands first.（他應該先洗手。）

(C)His hands are wet.（他的手是濕的。）

(D)His mother loves him very much.（他母親很愛他。）

答案：(C)

15. M: In China, water power is used to produce electricity, isn't it?

（男：在中國，水力被用來發電，不是嗎？）

W: Yes. But in some places, electricity is made by the wind.

（女：是的。但是在一些地方，是用風力發電。）

M: It is said that the energy from the sun can also produce electricity.

（男：據說太陽的能量也可以發電。）

W: That's cool. I will never be afraid of the lack of electricity.

（女：那真酷。我將永遠不怕缺乏電了。）

Q: Which power isn't mentioned in the dialogue?

（問題：哪一種能源在這段對話中沒有被提及？）

(A)Fire power.（火力。）　　　　　　(B)Solar energy.（太陽能。）

(C)Water power.（水力。）　　　　　(D)Wind power.（風力。）

答案：(A)

16. M: Rebecca, have you started to learn physics?（男：瑞貝卡，妳開始學物理了嗎？）

W: Sure. I had many lessons and I am interested in this subject.

（女：當然。我上了很多課並且我對此科目頗有興趣。）

M: Really? Then which section interests you most?

（男：真的？那麼哪個章節讓妳最感興趣？）

W: I saw some funny experiments about heat. And light makes me think of the mirror I look at every day. However, I have the most interest in electricity.

（女：我看到一些關於熱的好玩的實驗。光線讓我想到我每天看的鏡子。然而，我對電最有興趣。）

M: My favorite section is wave. It is powerful though it sometimes can not catch my eye.（男：我最喜歡的章節是波動。它很強大儘管它有時候不能吸引我注意。）

Q: What kind of funny experiments did the girl see in physics lessons?

（問題：這位女孩在物理課上看到怎樣的好玩實驗？）

(A)About wave.（關於波動。）　　　　(B)About electricity.（關於電。）

(C)About heat.（關於熱。）　　　　　(D)About light.（關於光線。）

答案：(C)

One day Richard Brody got a letter from a company in New York. The company had good news for Mr. Brody. "Congratulations!" the letter said. "You are the winner of a mini electronic piano! Please send us 10 dollars for shipping, and we will ship the piano to you."

有一天理查‧布羅迪收到一封從紐約一家公司來的信。這公司給布羅迪先生帶來好消息。「恭喜您！」這封信上說。「您是一台迷你電子鋼琴的得主！請給我們十美元的運費，我們將把這台鋼琴運給您。」

Mr. Brody read the letter very carefully and decided to mail the company 10 dollars for the piano. Two months later Mr. Brody received a box in the mail. It was his piano! He opened the box and found pieces of newspaper. He reached through the newspaper...and reached ...and reached. Finally, he felt something small and hard. He pulled out his piano. The piano was made of plastic and it was only five inches by two inches. It had 13 tiny buttons. When Mr. Brody pushed the buttons, the piano made a beeping sound. The piano costs 2 dollars in most stores.

布羅迪先生很仔細地讀了這封信後決定為這台鋼琴寄十美元給這家公司。兩個月後布羅迪先生在信件中收到一個盒子。是他的鋼琴！他打開盒子發現一些報紙碎片。他伸手穿過這些報紙...一直往下探...一直往下探。終於，他感受到某個又小又硬的東西。他將這鋼琴拉出來。這鋼琴是塑膠做的且它只有五吋乘兩吋大。它有十三個細小的按鍵。當布羅迪先生按這些按鍵，這鋼琴發出嗶嗶的聲音。這鋼琴在大多數商店賣二美元。

The company that sent Mr. Brody the piano was dishonest. Dishonest companies often do business by mail. They are very clever. They send letters and tell people that they own something. They also trick people with their advertising.

送這台鋼琴給布羅迪先生的這家公司並不誠實。不誠實的公司常常透過郵件做生意。他們很聰明。他們寄信告訴人們說他們擁有某些東西。他們也以他們的廣告欺騙人們。

Every year people in the USA send over 500 million dollars to dishonest companies. Perhaps Richard Brody can laugh because he spent only 10 for his "mini electronic piano". Some people send much more than 10 to dishonest companies.

每年在美國的人們寄超過五億美元給不誠實的公司。或許理查‧布羅迪可以大笑因為他為他的『迷你電子鋼琴』只寄了十元。有些人寄了遠超過十元給不誠實的公司。

17. One day, Richard Brody received a letter and a piano from a company in New York.（有一天，理查·布羅迪收到來自紐約一家公司的一封信和一台鋼琴。）

答案：(F 錯)

18. Richard Brody was clever enough not to send the 10 dollars to the company.（理查·布羅迪夠聰明而沒有寄十美元給該公司。）

答案：(F 錯)

19. The company really sent Richard Brody a piano that could make a sound.（該公司真的寄給理查布羅迪一台可以發出聲音的鋼琴。）

答案：(T 對)

20. The plastic piano cost 2 dollars more than the money Richard sent to the company.（這台塑膠鋼琴比理查寄給該公司的錢還要值多兩美元。）

答案：(F 錯)

21. Richard is just one of those who send money to dishonest companies every year.（理查只是每年寄錢給不誠實公司的人們當中的一位。）

答案：(T 對)

22. About 500 dollars are sent to such companies every year by Americans.（每年在美國大約五百美元被寄給這樣的公司。）

答案：(F 錯)

23. Actually, Richard belongs to the lucky as 10 dollars is after all a small amount.（事實上，理查算是幸運者，因為十美元畢竟是個小數目。）

答案：(T 對)

---

**IV、Listen to the passage and fill in the blanks with proper words.**（聽短文,用最恰當的詞填空,每格限填一詞）（共 7 分）

Communication, the first of the great uses for electricity, began with the telegraph invented by Samuel Morse around 1840, to be followed by the telephone, radio and television. Thomas Edison added lighting in 1880, which was soon followed by working electric motors and electric heating. Most recently have come electronics and the computer. In all electricity has basically changed the way we live.

溝通，電的偉大用途之首，開始於 1840 年前後薩謬爾摩爾斯發明的電報，接著有電話、收音機和電視。湯馬士愛迪生於 1880 年增加了照明，之後很快有工作的電動馬達和電暖器。最近則有了電子產品和電腦。整體上電在基本上改變了我們的生活方式。

As the practical uses for electricity grew, so did the need for its production. Edison built the first central power station and many power companies still use his name. Growth in giving out electricity led to the interconnection of the modern power grid, with power plants sometimes located over a thousand miles from users.

　　隨著電的實用性增長，對電的需求也成長。愛迪生建造了第一座中央發電站而很多電力公司仍然使用他的名字。給電量的增加也導致了現代化電力網路的相互連結，發電廠有時候位於距離用戶超過一千英里處。

　　Coal-fired steam and water power were the first sources of energy used to make electricity for business, later gas and oil were also burned to make electricity steam. Electricity has become the most important element in our lives.

　　煤炭火力蒸氣和水力是首先用來製造商業用電力的能量資源，後來瓦斯和石油也被燃燒來製造電力蒸氣。電已成為我們生活中最重要的元素。

- Samuel Morse invented the __24__ around 1840.
（薩繆爾摩爾斯於 1840 年前後發明了電報。）
- Thomas Edison invented lighting in __25__.
（湯馬士愛迪生於 1880 年發明了照明。）
- In all, the way we live has been __26__ by electricity.
（整體上，我們的生活方式被電改變了。）
- The practical uses for electricity as well as the __27__ for its production grew.（電的實用性還有對它生產量的需求一併成長。）
- Some power __28__ are located more than 1,000miles from us.
（有些發電廠位於距離我們超過一千英里處。）
- The __29__ sources of energy used to make electricity for business were coal-fired steam and water power.
（首先被用來製造商業用電的能量資源是煤炭火力蒸氣和水力。）
- Electricity has become the most essential __30__ in our daily life.
（電成為我門日常生活中不可或缺的元素。）

24. 答案：telegraph 電報
25. 答案：1880
26. 答案：changed 改變
27. 答案：need 需求
28. 答案：plants 廠
29. 答案：first 首先
30. 答案：element 元素

# 夏朵英文

## 全新英語聽力會考總複習原文及參考答案

# Unit 11

I、Listen and choose the right picture.（根據你聽到的內容,選出相應的圖片。）（6分）

1. Mrs. Wang is reading a story from the book to her children.
   （王太太正在給她的孩子們唸書上的一則故事。）
   答案：(D)

2. Danny is busy doing his homework and he is hard working.
   （丹尼正忙著做他的作業，他很用功。）
   答案：(F)

3. The naughty boy has grown up and he works as a pilot.
   （這頑皮的男孩已經長大做了飛行員的工作。）
   答案：(A)

4. A little girl is dancing around a tree as the tree was planted by her last year.
   （一位小女孩正繞著一棵樹跳舞，因為這樹就是她去年種下的。）
   答案：(B)

5. Daisy is thinking about why fish live in water.
   （黛西正想著為什麼魚兒在水中生活。）
   答案：(G)

6. Danny is walking freely on a sunny day.（丹尼在一個晴朗的日子自由地漫步著。）
   答案：(C)

7. W: Do you like reading newspapers or magazines?（女：你喜歡看報紙或是雜誌？）

   M: I am a football fan, so my favorite is the monthly football magazine called Football Family.

   （男：我是個足球迷，所以我的最愛是名為足球家族的足球雜誌月刊。）

   Q: How often is the magazine the man likes published?

   （問題：這位男士所喜歡的雜誌的出版頻率是？）

   (A)Every day.每天。)　　　　　　　　　(B)Once a week.一星期一次。)

   (C)Twice a month.每月兩次。)　　　　　(D)Every month. 每個月。)

   答案：(D)

8. W: Don't waste time on these newspapers. Please finish your homework as soon as possible.（女：別把時間浪費在這些報紙上。請盡速完成你的作業。）

   M: It's what my teacher asked me to do. I am looking for what I want.

   （男：這是我的老師要求我做的。我正在找我要的。）

   Q: Why does the boy spend time on the newspapers?

   （問題：為何這位男孩花時間在報紙上？）

   (A)Because his teacher wanted to borrow the newspapers.

   （因為他的老師想要借報紙。）

   (B)Because reading newspapers is his favorite activity.

   （因為閱讀報紙是他最喜歡的活動。）

   (C)Because it is his homework.（因為這是他的作業。）

   (D)Because he is looking for someone he wants to meet.

   （因為他在尋找他想要見的某個人。）

   答案：(C)

9. W: When should the postman send China Daily to my box?

   （女：郵差應該什麼時間把中國日報送到我的信箱？）

   M: Regularly at 3 p.m.（男：固定在下午三點。）

   W: But today he was half an hour late.（女：但是今天他晚了半小時。）

   M: On rainy days, postmen come a little bit late as they have to prepare some coverings.（男：在下雨天郵差會晚一點來，因為他們必須準備一些遮蓋物。）

   Q: When did the woman receive her newspaper today?

   （問題：這位女士今天幾點收到她的報紙？）

   (A)At 3:30.　　　　(B)At 4:00.　　　　(C)At 3:00.　　　　(D)She didn't get the newspaper.她沒有收到報紙。

   答案：(A)

10. W: Would you mind passing me that magazine?

    （女：你介意把那本雜誌遞給我嗎？）

M: Sure. By the way, how long have you stayed here reading?
（男：沒問題。對了，妳待在這裡閱讀了多久？）

W: All morning. It is quiet here and I enjoy the environment.
（女：整個上午。這裡很安靜且我喜歡這環境。）

Q: Where does this dialogue take place?（問題：這段會話在哪裡發生？）

(A)At a drug store.（在一間藥店。）

(B)In the boy's home.（在這位男孩的家中。）

(C)In a reading room.（在一間閱讀室。）

(D)In a dining room.（在飯廳。）

答案：(C)

11. W: Anything new?（女：有什麼新鮮事？）

M: It says on the front page that some Hong Kong people were killed by a policeman on a bus.（男：在頭版說有些香港人被一位警察在一輛巴士上殺害了。）

W: Oh, my god. Some good news for me?
（女：噢，我的天。可以給我一些好消息嗎？）

M: The forecast says that tomorrow a fierce typhoon will come and we won't go to school.（男：天氣預報說明天有一個強烈的颱風要來，我們不用去學校。）

Q: What is the boy doing now?（問題：這位男孩現在正在做什麼？）

(A)Watching TV.（看電視。）

(B)Reading a newspaper.（看報紙。）

(C)Listening to the radio.（聽收音機。）

(D)Chatting on the Internet.（在網路上聊天。）

答案：(B)

12. W: What's the matter with you?（女：你是怎麼了？）

M: I have a sore throat. What should I do then?（男：我喉嚨痛。那我該怎麼辦？）

W: Speak less. Having a rest is always more useful than medicine.
（女：少說話。休息一下總是比藥更有用。）

Q: What does the woman suggest the man do to treat his sore throat?
（問題：這位女士建議這位男士做什麼以治療他的喉嚨痛？）

(A)Take some medicine.（吃些藥。）　　　(B)Have a break.（休息一下。）

(C)Speak more.（多說話。）　　　(D)Go to the doctor's.（去看醫生。）

答案：(B)

13. W: I think I can win the game and nobody else can beat me.
（女：我想我可以贏這個比賽且沒人可以打敗我。）

M: It is easier said than done.（男：說比做容易。）

Q: What can we learn from the man?（問題：從這位男士我們可以得知？）

(A)The man agrees with the woman.（這位男士同意這位女士所說。）

(B)The man thinks it is impossible for the woman to win.
（這位男士認為這位女士不可能贏。）

(C)The man disagrees with the woman. （這位男士不同意這位女士所說。）

(D)The man thinks actions speak louder than words.

（這位男士認為事實勝於雄辯。）

答案：(D)

14. W: Have you ever seen a red pen? I left it on the desk.

（女：你有看到過一隻紅筆嗎？我把它留在書桌上。）

M: Is it a wooden one? I saw it on the shelf just now.

（男：是木頭的嗎？我剛剛才在架子上看到它。）

W: That's it. Can you put it in my pencil-box?

（女：就是它。你可以把它放到我的鉛筆盒裡嗎？）

M: OK, I will go and take it back. （男：好的，我會去把它拿回來。）

Q: Where did the girl leave the red pen? （問題：這位女孩把紅筆留在哪裡？）

(A)In the pencil-box. （在鉛筆盒裡。）　　(B)On the shelf. （在架子上。）

(C)On the desk. （在書桌上。）　　(D)In a wooden box. （在一個木盒子裡。）

答案：(C)

15. W: Would you like to have the flat with two bathrooms?

（女：你會想要有兩間浴室的公寓嗎？）

M: It will be more convenient. Is there a study in the flat?

（男：那樣會比較方便。在那間公寓裡有書房嗎？）

W: The balcony of the flat is big enough for you to leave space for study.

（女：這間公寓的陽台夠大到讓你留下空間來讀書。）

Q: What does the flat have? （問題：這間公寓有什麼？）

(A)A big balcony. （一個大陽台。）　　(B)A study. （一間書房。）

(C)Three bathrooms. （三間浴室。）　　(D)A small bathroom. （一間小臥室。）

答案：(A)

16. W: Sandy is a model student in our class and she likes writing diaries.

（女：珊蒂是我們班上的模範學生，她喜歡寫日記。）

M: How do you know that? I know Sandy does well in English.

（男：妳怎麼知道的？我知道珊蒂在英文上表現很好。）

W: Yes. Last time, she sang a lot of English songs for us and her voice was

wonderful. （女：是的。上一次，她為我們唱了很多英文歌，她的聲音很棒。）

Q: Which statement can't be used to describe Sandy?

（問題：何敘述不能用來形容珊蒂？）

(A)She is good at English. （她對英文很拿手。）

(B)She likes writing diaries. （她喜歡寫日記。）

(C)She enjoys writing songs. （她喜愛寫歌曲。）

(D)She sings English songs well. （她英文歌唱得好。）

答案：(C)

Bill was fourteen years old and in the ninth grade. He had a part-time job and he had to get up at five o'clock. He was a newspaper boy.

比爾十四歲,九年級。他有個兼職工作,他必須五點起床。他是個報童。

Each morning Bill left the house at five fifteen to go to the corner. The newspapers had been sent to the corner by a truck at midnight. He always rode a bike to take them.

每天早上比爾在五點十五分離家前往街角。報紙已在午夜時被一輛貨車送到街角。他總是騎腳踏車去拿。

In winter it was still dark when he got up, but during the rest of the year it was bright. Bill had to send the newspapers to people's houses in all kinds of weather. He tried to put each paper in the box where it would be kept safe from wind, rain or snow. His customers thought he did a good job. Sometimes they gave him tips.

在冬天他起床的時候天仍然是黑的,但在一年當中其他時候已經天亮。比爾必須在各種天氣之下把報紙送到家家戶戶。他試著把每份報紙放到信箱以在風雨或雪中保持安全。他的客戶認為他做得很好。有時候他們給他小費。

Bill made about ＄70 each month, and he had to save most of the money to go to college. He spent the rest on tapes and clothes. Once a month he had to get the money from his customers together. Since many of them worked during the day, Bill's father had to help him.

比爾每個月賺大約七十美元,他必須存下大部分的錢好上大學。他把剩餘的錢花在錄音帶和衣服上面。每個月一次他必須向他的客戶們一起收錢。由於他們當中很多人在白天工作,比爾的父親必須幫助他。

Bill had 70 customers, but he hoped to have more. If he got more customers, perhaps he could win a prize for being a very good newspaper boy. He wanted to win a visit to Europe, but he would be happy if he won a new bike.

比爾有七十位客戶,但他希望有更多。如果他有更多客戶,或許他能夠以成為很好的報童而得到一個獎。他想要贏得一次歐洲旅遊,但如果他贏得一台新的腳踏車他也會很高興。

17. Bill studied in Grade Nine and had to go to school very early.
（比爾就讀九年級,必須每天很早去學校。）
答案:(F 錯)

18. Newspapers are sent to the corner at midnight by truck.
（報紙在午夜時被卡車送到街角。）

答案：(T 對)

19. Bill's customers were pleased with Bill's job.
（比爾的客戶對比爾的工作感到滿意。）
答案：(T 對)

20. Bill saved all the money he earned as a newspaper boy for college expenses.
（比爾存下全部他當報童所賺的錢以作為大學費用。）
答案：(F 錯)

21. Sometimes Bill's father helped him send newspapers to people.
（有時候比爾的父親幫助他送報紙給人們。）
答案：(F 錯)

22. Bill was a boy who might enjoy listening to music.
（比爾可能是個喜愛聽音樂的男孩。）
答案：(T 對)

23. If Bill won a new bike instead of a trip to Europe, he would feel disappointed.
（如果比爾贏得一台新的腳踏車而不是歐洲旅遊，他會感到失望。）
答案：(F 錯)

---

**IV、Listen to the passage and fill in the blanks with proper words.**（聽短文,用最恰當的詞填空,每格限填一詞）（共 7 分）

A newspaper reporter's job can be very exciting. He meets different types of people and lives quite a busy life. He is looking for news all the time, and after some years he may get a desk job. Sometimes he may be so busy that he has no time to sleep well. And at other times, he may go on for days looking for news material.

報紙記者的工作可以是很刺激的。他遇到不同類型的人們並且過著頗為忙碌的生活。他隨時都在尋找新聞，幾年之後他可能得到一個辦公室的工作。有時候他可能忙碌到沒時間好好睡覺。而在其他時間，他可能持續數日尋找新聞的材料。

In the beginning, a reporter has to cover a very wide area. After the early years he becomes more specialized in his work. Some reporters may become so specialized that they are asked only to write in a special area. Some newspapers have book reviews. A reporter may read the latest books and then write reviews on the ones he likes. There are those who write on films, and they can see the films even before they are shown in the cinema.

在開始的時候，一名記者必須涵蓋很廣的範圍。初期的幾年後他變得在他的工作上更專精。有些記者可能變成專精到被要求只寫一個特殊領域以內的東西。有些報紙有書籍評論。記者可能閱讀最新的書籍然後對他所喜歡的寫下評論。也有人寫關於電影的，他們甚至可以在戲院上映之前看電影。

A reporter's job can also be very dangerous. If there is a war, they may get hurt or even be killed. Three years ago there was a reporter whose camera was broken by a group of men, because they were angry with him for taking pictures of them. Dangerous or not, one thing is certain — a reporter's job is never uninteresting!

記者的工作也可以是很危險的。如果有戰爭，他們可能受傷或甚至喪生。三前年有一位記者的相機被一群人弄壞，因為他拍他們的照片使他們生氣。無論是否危險，有一件事是肯定的 — 記者的工作絕對不會無趣！

- A newspaper reporter will __24__ different kinds of people in the job.
  （報紙記者在工作上會遇到不同種類的人們。）
- A reporter may have a __25__ job after looking for news everywhere for some years.（記者在到處找尋新聞數年之後可能有辦公室的工作。）
- A reporter's job ranges from covering a __26__ area to a special one.
  （記者的工作從涵蓋廣大範圍到專精特殊領域有很多種類。）
- A reporter writes book reviews after reading the __27__ books.
  （記者在閱讀最新的書之後寫書籍評論。）
- A reporter always watches movies __28__ movies are on at cinemas.
  （記者總是在戲院上映之前看電影。）
- A group of tough guys __29__ a reporter's camera when they were taken pictures of 3 years ago.
  （三年前當一群頑強的傢伙們被拍照時弄壞了一名記者的相機。）
- A reporter's job is both exciting and dangerous but never ever __30__.
  （記者的工作是既刺激又危險，但是絕對不會無趣。）

24. 答案：meet（遇到）
25. 答案：desk（書桌）
26. 答案：wide（廣大）
27. 答案：latest（最新）
28. 答案：before（之前）
29. 答案：broke（弄壞）
30. 答案：uninteresting（無趣）

# 夏朵英文
## 全新英語聽力會考總複習原文及參考答案
# Unit 12

---

I、Listen and choose the right picture.（根據你聽到的內容,選出相應的圖片。）（6分）

A     B     C

D    E    F    G

1. The story tells us something about an accident caused by a typhoon.
   （這故事告訴我們關於一場颱風造成的意外的一些事情。）
   答案：(A)

2. Two children read the magazine attentively as it was about basketball.
   （兩個小孩很專心地讀了那本雜誌因為它是關於籃球。）
   答案：(D)

3. It is reported that many high buildings will be put up in this small city.
   （消息指出很多高建築物將在這小都市中建起。）
   答案：(B)

4. This article describes a strange flower that can change its color.
   （這篇文章敘述一種可以變換顏色的奇怪花朵。）
   答案：(F)

5. Jane is a hardworking student. Asking and answering is what she likes.
   （珍是個用功的學生。問與答是她所喜歡的。）
   答案：(G)

6. Tom has learnt to play the violin for three years.（湯姆學拉小提琴三年了。）
   答案：(C)

7. M: Alice, does Mrs. Wang live on the second floor?
（男：愛麗絲，王太太是住在二樓嗎？）

W: She lives three floors higher. But Mrs. Lin does.
（女：她住得更高三層。但是林太太住二樓。）

M: I just came from Mrs. Yao's apartment and I was on the fourth floor. Now I am going to visit Mrs. Wang.
（男：我剛剛從姚太太的公寓出來，我剛剛在四樓。現在我要去拜訪王太太。）

Q: How can the boy reach the destination?（問題：這位男孩要如何達到目的地。）

(A)Go 1 floor higher.（上一層樓。）　　　(B)Go 3 floors higher.（上三層樓。）

(C)Go 2 floors lower.（下兩層樓。）　　　(D)Go 3 floors lower.（下三層樓。）

答案：(A)

8. M: What a nice beach it is!（男：多麼讚的一片沙灘啊！）

W: Look, the boy in green is making sandcastles and the boy in white is collecting shells. How lovely they are!（女：看啊，穿綠衣服的男孩正在堆沙堡而穿白衣服的男孩正在收集貝殼。他們多可愛。）

M: The magic beach makes it. Let's take a sunbath and have a rest.
（男：是魔術般的海灘造成的。讓我們做個日光浴休息一下吧。）

Q: What is the boy in white doing at the beach?
（問題：穿白衣服的男孩在沙灘上做什麼？）

(A)Having a rest.（休息。）　　　(B)Taking a sunbath.（做沙浴。）

(C)Collecting shells.（收集貝殼。）　　　(D)Making sandcastles.（堆沙堡。）

答案：(C)

9. M: What's up, Jane?（男：怎麼了，珍？）

W: Who broke my glass? The milk is everywhere.
（女：誰把我的玻璃杯打破了？牛奶灑得到處都是。）

M: I saw Coco playing around. Er...Now I know why I heard the bark.
（男：我看到可可在附近玩。呃...現在我知道為何我聽到狗吠。）

Q: Who is Coco?（問題：誰是可可？）

(A)A pet cat.（一隻寵物貓。）

(B)A naughty kid.（一位頑皮的小孩。）

(C)A friend of theirs.（他們的一位朋友。）

(D)A pet dog.（一隻寵物狗。）

答案：(D)

10. M: Tomorrow should be a bad day.（男：明天應該是個壞天氣。）

W: Why? The forecast says it will be sunny.（女：為何？氣象預報說會出太陽。）

M: Didn't you see the dark clouds such as the math test, the physics quiz and the Chinese exam?

（男：你沒看到例如數學測驗、物理問答和中文考試這樣的烏雲嗎？）

Q: Why does the boy think it will be a bad day tomorrow?（問題：為何這位男孩認為明天會是個壞天氣？）

(A)Because the forecast tells it to him.（因為氣象預報這樣告訴他。）

(B)Because he will have many tests.（因為他會有很多考試。）

(C)Because it is going to rain.（因為將要下雨。）

(D)Because the boy is poor at all subjects.（因為這位男孩全部科目都很爛。）

答案：(B)

11. M: What time is it now? It is three thirty-five by my watch.

（男：現在幾點？照我的錶是三點三十五分。）

W: Your watch is fifteen minutes slow. Please check it later.

（女：你的錶慢了十五分鐘。之後請檢查它。）

M: It's very kind of you.（男：妳人真好。）

Q: What time is it now?（問題：現在幾點？）

(A)3:20.　　　　(B)3:50.　　　　(C)2:45.　　　　(D)3:25.

答案：(B)

12. M: Time for breakfast. What do you want, bread with jam or bread with butter?

（男：早餐時間嘍。妳想要什麼，麵包配果醬或是麵包配奶油？）

W: Can I have the toast with butter?（女：我可以要點土司麵包配奶油嗎？）

M: Sure. A minute, please.（男：當然。請等一下。）

Q: What does the lady want to have for breakfast?（問題：這位淑女早餐想吃什麼？）

(A)Toast with jam.（土司配果醬。）

(B)Bread with jam.（麵包配果醬。）

(C)Bread with butter.（麵包配奶油。）

(D)Toast with butter.（土司麵包配奶油。）

答案：(D)

13. M: Where is Canada located, Tom?（男：加拿大位在哪裡，湯姆？）

W: It is located in the center of America.（女：它位於美洲的中間。）

M: I'm sorry. Please check it on the map. Jane, can you tell us the right answer?

（男：抱歉。請在地圖上確認。珍，妳可以告訴我們正確的答案嗎？）

Q: Where does this conversation most probably take place?

（問題：這段對話最有可成是在哪裡發生。）

(A)In a bookstore.（在一間書店。）　　　(B)In a library.（在圖書館。）

(C)In the classroom.（在教室裡。）　　　(D)In a map shop.（在一間地圖店。）

答案：(C)

14. M: Mike's plan for his summer vacation is wonderful. He plans to visit France.

（男：麥克的暑假計畫很讚。他計畫造訪法國。）

W: That's cool. I decide to read some books about travelling around the world.

（女：那真酷。我決定要讀一些關於環遊世界的書。）

M: I think I can be a part-time tour guide and welcome the foreigners to our city.

（男：我認為我可以當一個兼職導遊來歡迎外國人到我們的城市。）

Q: What are they talking about?（問題：他們在談論什麼？）

(A)Traveling in the world.（環遊世界。）

(B)Their summer holiday.（他們的暑假。）

(C)A romantic country — France.（一個浪漫的國家－法國。）

(D)Jobs they do.（他們所做的工作。）

答案：(B)

15. M: When will you leave for Shanghai?（男：妳什麼時候要出發去上海？）

W: I had decided to go there the day after tomorrow.（女：我決定後天去那邊。）

M: What happened then?（男：發生了什麼事？）

W: My boss gave me one more day to make preparations.

（女：我老闆多給我一天可以做準備。）

M: So you will go there on Friday.（男：所以妳星期五去那邊。）

W: Yes, that's it.（女：是的，就是。）

Q: What day is it today?（問題：今天星期幾？）

(A)Friday.（星期五。） (B)Thursday.（星期四。）

(C)Wednesday.（星期三。） (D)Tuesday.（星期二。）

答案：(C)

16. M: Cindy, you are late.（男：辛蒂，妳遲到了。）

W: I'm so sorry about that. My mom is badly ill and I have to buy her some medicine.（女：為此我非常抱歉。我媽媽病得很重，我必須買些藥給她。）

M: I'm sorry to hear that. Why not take her to hospital?

（男：聽到這消息我很遺憾。為何不帶她去醫院？）

W: My mom didn't want me to miss the lessons.（女：我媽媽不想要我錯過課堂。）

Q: Why was Cindy late? （問題：辛蒂為何遲到？）

(A)She went to buy some medicine.（她去買一些藥。）

(B)She took her mom to hospital.（她帶她媽媽去醫院。）

(C)She planned to miss the lessons.（她計畫好錯過課堂。）

(D)She was badly ill.（她病得很重。）

答案：(A)

Ⅲ、Listen to the passage and tell whether the following statements are true or false.

（判斷下列句子是否符合你聽到的短文內容,符合用 T 表示,不符合用 F 表示）(7分)

Baseball is a very popular sport in America. Many people enjoy this game. It is sometimes called the most popular game in America. Many Americans think that it is their national sport.

棒球在美國是一項很受歡迎的運動。很多人喜歡這種球賽。它有時候被稱為美國最受歡迎的球賽。很多美國人認為這是他們的國家運動。

Baseball is a game played outside between two teams of nine players each, in which players try to get points by hitting a ball and running around four bases. Different players have different jobs when the team is on the field. Each team must try to get more points than the other team. When a player hits the ball and then runs around the playing field to each of the four bases, he will get a point.

棒球是一種兩個各九人的團隊在戶外一起參與的球賽,在此球賽中球員試著以擊球和在四個壘之間跑來得分。當球隊在球場上,不同的球員有不同的職責。每隊都必須試著比另一隊得到更多分。當一位球員擊球然後繞著球場逐一跑上四個壘,他就會得一分。

A good baseball player must do two things well. First, he must hit the ball well when it is his turn. Second, he must catch and throw the ball well. When his team is on the field, he can keep the other team from winning.

一位好的棒球選手一定要把兩件事做好。第一,當輪到他的時候他必須把球打擊得好。第二,他必須把球接得好和傳得好。當他的球隊在球場上,他可以防止其他球隊贏球。

Of course, there are some good things about baseball. You don't have to miss baseball games during the summer months. The weather is warm. It is happy to sit outside for a few hours and watch a game. You don't have to pay too much money for the baseball game, and then you can have a very good time.

當然,棒球有一些優點。在夏天的月份裡你不要錯過棒球賽。天氣溫暖。坐在戶外幾個小時看球賽頗快樂。你不用付太多錢看棒球賽,就可以很盡興。

17. All the Americans think baseball is their national sport.
（每個美國人都認為棒球是他們的國家運動。）
答案：(F 錯)

18. A baseball game is played by altogether 18 players.
（一場棒球賽是由總共十八位球員進行。）
答案：(T 對)

19. There are five bases for players to run around in a baseball game.
（在一場棒球賽有五個壘讓球員繞著跑答案。）
答案：(F 錯)

20. The team can get one point by hitting the ball.（球隊可藉由擊球得分。）
答案：(F 錯)

21. Good baseball players catch the balls better than throw them.
（好的棒球選手接球比傳球好。）

答案：(F 錯)

22. There are few baseball games in summer as the weather is too hot.
（夏天有很少的棒球賽因為天氣太熱了。）

答案：(F 錯)

23. A baseball game can take several hours.（一場棒球賽可以打幾個小時。）

答案：(T 對)

---

**IV、Listen to the passage and fill in the blanks with proper words.**（聽短文,用最恰當的詞填空,每格限填一詞）（共 7 分）

International Pen Friends allows students to learn about countries and cultures at first hand by writing letters to someone of their own age. IPF is also a great way to learn a new language, or to make some friends.

國際筆友會（IPF）讓學生可以透過寫信給同年齡的人直接學到各國及其文化。IPF 也是個學習新語言或是交些朋友的好方法。

International Pen Friends was founded in Dublin, Ireland on 7 April 1967. The aim of IPF is to give people of all ages from every country the opportunity to get pen friends and friendship through letter writing. IPF does not use the Internet to match pen friends. IPF wants to keep the art of letter writing alive and to use that form of communication to encourage worldwide friendship. Since 1967, International Pen Friends has provided more than one and a half million people aged from 7 to 80 with pen friends.

國際筆友 1967 年 4 月 7 日成立於愛爾蘭的都柏林。IPF 的目標是透過寫信給每個國家所有年齡的人交筆友和得到友誼的機會。IPF 不用網際網路來媒合筆友。IPF 希望維持寫信的藝術存活下去並且用那種溝通的形式來促進世界性的友誼。從 1967 年起，國際筆友提供筆友給超過一百五十萬人，年齡從七歲到八十歲。

Is it possible to join IPF individually, with a friend or as part of a school class or youth group? The person who wants to be a member of IPF should provide his or her personal information such as the name, the age, the nationality and hobbies. Once the person becomes the member of IPF, his／her information will be given to other members of the club. This system enables members to choose their pen friends by writing introductory letters to the people, and to receive surprise introductory letters from other members.

個人、和一個朋友一起、以學校班級的一部分或年輕社群的一部分都可能加入 IPF 嗎？想要成為 IPF 會員的人應提供他或她的個人資料例如名字、年齡、國籍和嗜好。一但這個人成為 IPF 的會員，他／她的資料將被給予俱樂部中的其他會員。這個系統讓會員們可以透過寫介紹信給人們來選擇他們的筆友，和意外地收到其他會員的介紹信。

- IPF is a great way to learn a new __24__ as well.
  （IPF 也是學習新語言的好方法。）
- On 7 April, __25__, International Pen Friends was founded in Dublin, Ireland.
  （在 1967 年 4 月 7 日，國寄筆友創立於愛爾蘭的都柏林。）
- IPF feels like keeping the art of letter writing __26__.
  （IPF 覺得要維持寫信的藝術活下去。）
- IPF has __27__ pen friends for more than one and a half million people aged from 7 to 80.
  （IPF 提供筆有給超過一百五十萬人，年齡從七歲到八十歲。）
- A member of IPF should give his or her personal __28__.
  （IPF 的會員應提供他或她的個人資料。）
- The name, the age, the nationality, __29__ and other things are given to IPF.
  （名字、年齡、國籍、嗜好和其他東西被提供給 IPF。）
- This system makes it __30__ for members to choose their pen friends by writing introductory letters to the people.
  （這個系統讓會員們可以透過寫介紹信給人們來選擇他們的筆友。）

24. 答案：language（語言）
25. 答案：1967
26. 答案：alive（活著）
27. 答案：provided（提供）
28. 答案：information（資料）
29. 答案：hobbies（嗜好）
30. 答案：possible（可能）

# 夏朵英文

# Unit 13

---

I、Listen and choose the right picture.（根據你聽到的內容,選出相應的圖片。）（6分）

A　　　　　　　B　　　　　　　C

D　　　　　　　E　　　　　　　F　　　　　　　G

1.  Sammy dreams of traveling around the world with his pet dog Charlie.
    （桑密夢想著和他的寵物狗查理一起到世界各地旅行。）
    答案：(F)

2.  This article is about a popular baseball player who is always kind to his fans.
    （這篇文章是關於一位受歡迎的棒球選手，他總是對他的球迷很好。）
    答案：(G)

3.  The well-known actress sent his son to school and said goodbye to him.
    （這位知名的女星送她兒子去上學並和他說再見。）
    答案：(E)

4.  Roy and Ray want to find a judge as they plan to have a tennis match.
    （羅伊和雷想要找個裁判，因為他們計劃打一場網球賽。）
    答案：(C)

5.  Alice asks Jane about the riddle in the newspaper, but she can't work it out.
    （愛莉斯問珍關於報紙裡的謎語，但是她解不出來。）
    答案：(B)

6.  Tommy asks his mother to see his report while she is cooking dinner.
    （湯米要求他母親看他的的報告，當她正在煮晚餐的時候。）

答案：(A)

7. M: There will be a fireworks show in the Century Park tomorrow. Would you like to go with me?（男：明天在世紀公園會有一場煙火秀。妳想跟我去嗎？）

W: I'd love to. But I have to visit my grandma with my aunt.
（女：我很想。但是我必須和我阿姨一起去拜訪我祖母。）

M: That's all right. Say hello to your grandma for me.
（男：沒關係。幫我像妳的祖母問好。）

Q: What will the girl do tomorrow?（問題：這位女孩明天會做什麼？）

(A)Visit her aunt.（拜訪她的阿姨。）　　　(B)See her grandma.（去看她祖母。）

(C)Watch the show.（看那場秀。）　　　(D)Go to the park.（去公園。）

答案：(B)

8. M: Jane, have you got your exam report?（男：珍，妳拿到妳的成績單了嗎？）

W: Yes, Dad. I will show it to you.（女：是的，爸。我會拿給你看。）

M: OK. You get A grades in math and physics. Congratulations!
（男：好。妳在數學和物理拿到 A。恭喜！）

W: Thanks, Dad. But I get C in English and B in Chinese. What should I do?
（女：謝謝爸。但是我在英文拿到 C 而中文拿到 B。我該怎麼辦？）

M: Don't worry. To read more is always useful.（男：別擔心。多讀書總是有用的。）

Q: Which subjects is the girl weak in?（問題：這位女孩弱在哪一科？）

(A)Math and physics.（數學和物理。）

(B)Physics and Chinese.（物理和中文。）

(C)English and math.（英文和數學。）

(D)English and Chinese.（英文和中文。）

答案：(D)

9. M: Excuse me, is Mrs. Wang at the office?（男：請問，王太太在辦公室嗎？）

W: She has gone to London. She won't be back until next week.
（女：她去倫敦了。她直到下星期都不會回來。）

M: I see. May I meet her next Friday?
（男：我明白了。我可以下星期五和她見面嗎？）

W: You can call again next Thursday.（女：你可以下星期四再打電話來。）

Q: When will Mrs. Wang return?（問題：王太太什麼時候會回來？）

(A)Next Monday.（下星期一。）　　　(B)Next Friday.（下星期五。）

(C)Next Wednesday.（下星期三。）　　　(D)Next Thursday.（下星期四。）

答案：(D)

10. M: How can I get to the zoo?（男：我怎樣可以到動物園？）

W: You'd better not drive there as the gate is far from the parking lot.
（女：你最好不要開車去那裡，因為大門離停車場很遠。）

M: Can I call a taxi?（男：我可以叫計程車嗎？）

W: What's the difference? The underground will go right there.
（女：那有什麼兩樣？地鐵會直達那邊。）

Q: How does the woman suggest the man go to the zoo?
（問題：這位女士建議這位男士如何去動物園？）

(A)By metro.（搭地鐵。） (B)By taxi.（搭計程車。）
(C)By car.（開車。） (D)On foot.（走路。）

答案：(A)

11. M: Who is that woman?（男：那位女士是誰？）

W: Which woman?（女：哪位女士？）

M: The one with long hair.（男：那位有長頭髮的。）

W: She is the class teacher of Class Four and the other one with short hair is the class teacher of Class Ten. They are both 37 years old.（女：她是四班的班導師，而另一位短頭髮的是十班的班導師。她們都是三十七歲。）

Q: Which statement is not true?（問題：哪個說明是不正確的？）

(A)The woman with long hair is 37 years old.（長頭髮的女士是三十七歲。）
(B)The woman with short hair is a teacher.（短頭髮的女士是一位老師。）
(C)The class teacher of Class Ten has long hair.（十班的班導師有長頭髮。）
(D)The class teacher of Class Four is 37 years old.（四班的班導師是三十七歲。）

答案：(C)

12. M: What's this? It looks so strange.（男：這是什麼？它看起來好怪。）

W: So strange? It is worth 1 million dollars.（女：好怪嗎？它值一百萬美金。）

M: How do you know that?（男：妳怎麼知道？）

W: It is a bowl made of special stone one thousand years ago.
（女：這是一個一千年前以特殊石材製造的碗。）

M: What a pity it is that my father isn't here now. He has much interest in ancient things.（男：我父親現在不在這裡真可惜。他對古老的東西很有興趣。）

Q: Where does this dialogue take place?（問題：這段對話在哪裡發生？）

(A)In a bookstore.（在書店。） (B)At the bank.（在銀行。）
(C)In the post office.（在郵局。） (D)In a museum.（在博物館。）

答案：(D)

13. M: Mary, can you tell me Mrs. Lin's cell phone number?
（男：瑪莉，妳可以告訴我林太太的行動電話號碼嗎？）

W: OK. It is 13817273749.（女：好的。是 13817273749。）

M: Thank you so much. Er, wait, why does the receiver say that the number doesn't exist?（男：多謝妳。呃，等等，為何電話那頭說此號碼不存在？）

W: Let me check. I am so sorry that the second seven should be five.

（女：讓我檢查一下。我很抱歉，第二個七應該是五。）

Q: What is the right number of Mrs. Lin's cell phone?

（問題：林太太行動電話的正確號碼是？）

(A)13815273749.　　(B)13817253749.　(C)13817273549.　(D)13817273745.

答案：(B)

14. M: Rebecca, how about your Math exam? You are always the top in our class.

（男：瑞貝卡，妳數學考得怎麼樣？妳總是我們班上的第一。）

W: Thanks. But this time I made three mistakes in Choice which cost me two points each because I didn't pay attention to the definitions in the book.

（女：謝謝。但是這次我在選擇題犯了三個錯，每題讓我失去兩分，因為我沒有注意書上的定義。）

M: It's just because of your carelessness. Forget it and I think you will soon get 100 again.（男：只是因為妳的不小心。忘了吧，我想妳很快就會再次考一百分。）

W: I will work harder. Let's wait and see.（女：我會更用功。讓我們等著瞧。）

Q: What is the score of Rebecca's math exam?（問題：瑞貝卡的數學考試得幾分？）

(A)94 points.（九十四分）　　　　　　(B)96 points.（九十六分）

(C)98 points.（九十八分）　　　　　　(D)100 points.（一百分）

答案：(A)

15. M: What's the name of the program?（男：這節目名稱是什麼？）

W: It's called "Day Day Up".（女：它叫作「日日升」。）

M: But why do I often see lots of stars giving performances on the stage?

（男：但是為什麼我常常看到很多明星在舞台上表演？）

W: I think they also represent part of the culture and we can learn something as well.（女：我想他們也代表文化的一部分而我們也可以學點什麼。）

Q: What are they talking about?（問題：他們在談論什麼？）

(A)How to study well.（如何把書念好。）

(B)Super stars.（超級明星。）

(C)A TV program.（一個電視節目。）

(D)Daily news.（每日新聞。）

答案：(C)

16. M: Where would you like to further your study?（男：妳想在哪裡繼續妳的學業？）

W: France is famous for art while in London, I can learn about economy.

（女：法國在藝術方面很有名，而在倫敦我可以學經濟方面。）

M: Last time I was told that you were interested in financial analysis.

（男：上次我聽說妳對金融分析有興趣。）

W: Yes. If I decide to learn it, I have to choose Harvard University.

（女：對。如果我決定學這個，我必須選哈佛大學。）

Q: If the girl wants to learn something related to finance, where should she go to further her study?（問題：如果這位女孩想學和金融有關的一些東西，她應該

去哪裡繼續她的學業？）

(A)England.（英國）　　　　　　　　(B)France.（法國）

(C)America.（美國）　　　　　　　　(D)Germany.（德國）

答案：(C)

---

**Ⅲ Listen to the passage and tell whether the following statements are true or false.**

（判斷下列句子是否符合你聽到的短文內容,符合用 T 表示,不符合用 F 表示）(7 分)

---

A young traveler was exploring the Alps. He came upon a big empty land. It was like the wasteland. It was the kind of place you hurry away from.

一位年輕的旅人正在探索阿爾卑斯山脈。他來到一大片空地上。它像是一片荒原。它是那種你會快快離開的地方。

Then, suddenly, the young traveler stopped dead to have a rest. In the middle of this big wasteland was a bent-over old man. On his back was a bag of seeds. In his hand was a four-foot-long iron pipe.

然後，忽然，這位年輕旅人停下來靜止著休息。在這一大片荒原中間有一位彎著腰的老人。在他的背上是一袋種子。在他手裡是一根四尺長的鐵管。

The old man was using the iron pipe to dig holes in the ground. Then from the bag he would take a seed and put it in the hole. Later the old man told the traveler, "I've planted 100,000 seeds. Perhaps only one tenth of them will grow." The old man's wife and son had died, and this was how he chose to spend his final years. "I want to do something useful," he said.

這位老人正在用這根鐵管往地上挖洞。然後他會從袋子裡拿出一顆種子放到洞裡。之後這位老人告訴這位旅人，「我種了十萬顆種子。或許它們當中只有十分之一會長出來。」這位老人的妻子和兒子已經死了，而這是他選擇度過餘生的方式。「我想要做些有用的事，」他說。

Twenty-five years later the now-not-as-young traveler returned to the same place. What he saw amazed him. He could not believe his own eyes. The land was covered with a beautiful forest two miles wide and five miles long. Birds were singing, animals were playing, and wild flowers perfumed the air.

二十五年後不再那麼年輕的旅人回到了同一個地方。他所看到的讓他驚奇。他無法相信他的眼睛。這塊地被兩英里寬五英里長美麗的森林覆蓋著。鳥兒在唱歌，動物在嬉戲，而野花們使空氣芳香。

The traveler stood there recalling the wilderness that once was; a beautiful forest stood there now — all because someone cared.

這位旅人站在那裡回想著曾經一度的荒廢景像；現在一片美麗的森林矗立在那裡 — 全因為某個人關心。

---

17. A young traveler lost his way on the Alps.

（一位年輕的旅人在阿爾卑斯山脈迷路了。）

答案：(F 錯)

18. An old man with magic power saved the traveler's life.
（一位有魔法的老人救了這位旅人的命。）
答案：(F 錯)

19. The old man used a metal pipe to dig a hole where the seed could be put.
（這位老人用一根金屬管在要放種子的地方挖洞。）
答案：(T 對)

20. The old man lived alone and wanted to do something useful.
（這位老人獨居，想要做些有用的事。）
答案：(T 對)

21. The traveler came to the place again twenty years later.
（這位旅人二十年後再次來到這個地方。）
答案：(F 錯)

22. The wasteland disappeared and the land looked beautiful and smelt nice.
（荒原消失了，這片地看起來美麗且氣味芬芳。）
答案：(T 對)

23. The writer saw the 100,000 trees and was thankful to the old man.
（筆者看到十萬棵樹，對老人很感激。）
答案：(F 錯)

---

**IV、Listen to the passage and fill in the blanks with proper words.**（聽短文,用最恰當的詞填空,每格限填一詞）（共7分）

The tourist guide book has gone digital in Japan. New technology that sends data to a hand held screen is being tried in Tokyo. It can tell you where you are, the history of landmarks and buildings, and the shopping secrets of the city.

在日本觀光導遊書籍已進入數位化。可以把新資料送到一個手持螢幕的新科技已在東京試用。它可以告訴你在哪裡、地標和建築物的歷史，還有此都市的購物祕訣。

Tokyo is a busy international city. But it's also easy to feel puzzled by all the buildings, shops, neon lights and crowded streets around you.

東京是個忙碌的國際都市。但也很容易感到被你周圍所有的建築物、店鋪、霓虹燈和擁擠街道所迷惑的地方。

But now help is at hand, in the form of a small device. Like a smart phone, it can receive useful information on your exact location, where to eat and where to shop.

但是現在幫助就在手邊，以一個小裝置的型態。像個智慧型手機，它可以接收關於你精確的所在地的有用資訊，去哪裡吃、去哪裡購物。

People can walk through the city and learn about it as they go.

人們可以走路穿越此都市並在行動中了解它。

And locals can have some fun with it too.

當地人也可以從它得到一些樂趣。

One tourist said, "I think it's useful and it's faster than a normal map and it's easy to use. I think it would be better to use this tool in all of the city and not just here in the center."

一位觀光客說，「我認為它很有用而且它比普通地圖更快又易於使用。我認為在整個都市都用這個工具會比較好，而不是只在位居中心的這裡。」

The technology is being developed by the Tokyo Government.

此科技正被東京政府開發中。

"Anyone, any time, anywhere" is the project motto and that's what the system delivers.

「任何人、任何時候、在任何地方」是此企劃的座右銘，正是這個系統所給予的。

● In Japan, a new electronic __24__ book has appeared.
（在日本，一個新的電子導遊書已出現。）

● The books tell where you are, the history of landmarks and buildings, and the shopping __25__ of the city.
（這些書告訴你在哪裡、地標和建築物的歷史、和此都市的購物祕訣。）

● All the buildings, shops, neon lights and __26__ streets around you make you confused in Japan.
（在日本，你周圍所有的建築物、店鋪、霓虹燈和擁擠的街道使你迷惑。）

● The electronic book looks like a smart __27__ in appearance.
（這電子書在外觀上看起來像個智慧型手機。）

● Travelers as well as __28__ people can have some fun with the newly-produced book.
（旅人和當地人也都可以從這個新生產的書得到一些樂趣。）

● The book is more useful and __29__ than a normal map.
（這本書更有用且比普通地圖更快。）

● What the system __30__ is "Anyone, any time, anywhere".
（這個系統所給予的是「任何人、任何時候、在任何地方」。）

24. 答案：guide（導遊）
25. 答案：secrets（祕訣）
26. 答案：crowded（擁擠）
27. 答案：phone（電話）
28. 答案：local（當地）
29. 答案：faster（更快）
30. 答案：delivers（給予）

Ⅰ、Listen and choose the right picture.（根據你聽到的內容,選出相應的圖片。）（6分）

A      B      C

D      E      F      G

1. The fun the boy is having makes Mr. White never melt.
   （這位男孩的樂趣使白先生永遠不融化。）
   答案：(E)

2. The more members, the more difficulties. The higher, the better.
   （成員越多，困難越多。越高越好。）
   答案：(D)

3. Drums bothering you make you cry while drums played by you make you smile.
   （鼓吵到你使你哭，而你打的鼓則使你微笑。）
   答案：(G)

4. The wind blows fiercely, and the leaves fly freely. Winter is soon here.
   （風猛烈地吹，樹葉自由地飛。冬天很快就要到了。）
   答案：(B)

5. Water, the killer of thirst. Water, the source of life.
   （水，口渴的殺手。水，生命的根源。）
   答案：(C)

6. Lying quietly, sleeping. Thinking deeply, dreaming.
   （靜靜地躺著，睡著。深深地思考，夢著。）

答案：(A)

---

II、Listen to the dialogue and choose the best answer to the question. （根據你聽到的對話和問題，選出最恰當的答案。）（10分）

7. M: When will your father come back, Jane?（男：妳父親何時會回來，珍？）

W: Yesterday he told me that he had bought the train ticket for the next day.

（女：昨天他告訴我說他買了次日的火車票。）

M: How time flies! I will see him soon. Let's drive to pick him up.

（男：時光飛逝！我很快會見到他了。讓我們開車去接他吧。）

Q: How will the girl's father come back?（問題：這位女孩的父親將如何回來？）

(A)By plane.（搭飛機。） (B)By car.（開車。）

(C)By train.（搭火車。） (D)By bicycle.（騎腳踏車。）

答案：(C)

8. M: How much is the cabbage?（男：包心菜多少錢？）

W: It used to cost 3 yuan per kilo. But now I can give you 50% discount.

（女：它曾經賣一公斤三元。但現在我可以給你打五折。）

M: Really? May I have 3 kilos?（男：真的？我可以買三公斤嗎？）

W: Sure. I will weigh for you.（女：當然。我來幫你秤。）

Q: How much does the man pay for the cabbage altogether?

（問題：這位男士總共為包心菜付多少錢？）

(A)9 yuan.（九元） (B)5 yuan.（五元）

(C)1.5 yuan.（一元五毛） (D)4.5 yuan.（四元五毛）

答案：(D)

9. M: Rose, would you please tell your monitor, Jack, to come here for a meeting?

（男：蘿絲，可否請妳告訴你們的班長傑克過來開會？）

W: Of course, Roy. But we have held a new election and he didn't win more support than Jason.

（女：當然，羅伊。但是我們舉辦了新的選舉而他沒有比傑森贏得更多支持。）

M: OK. Inform the new one, please.（男：好。通知新的那位，麻煩妳。）

W: I will.（女：我會的。）

Q: Who will go to have a meeting?（問題：誰會去開會？）

(A)Jason.（傑森） (B)Rose.（蘿絲） (C)Roy.（羅伊） (D)Jack.（傑克）

答案：(A)

10. M: We learned a story from The Epics of Homer.

（男：我們從荷馬的史詩中學到一個故事。）

W: Oh, was Homer a great poet in ancient Egypt or Rome?

（女：喔，荷馬是古埃及或是羅馬的一位偉大詩人吧？）

M: Neither. He lived in ancient Greece.（男：都不是。他活在古希臘。）

W: I am sorry. I just know something about ancient China but nothing about them.（女：真抱歉。我只知道一些關於古中國的事而對他們我一無所知。）

Q: Where did Homer come from according to the dialogue?
（問題：根據這段對話，荷馬是從哪裡來的？）

(A)Ancient Egypt.（古埃及。） (B)Ancient China.（古中國。）
(C)Ancient Greece.（古希臘。） (D)Ancient Rome.（古羅馬。）

答案：(C)

11. M: Rebecca, what are you going to do this afternoon?
（男：瑞貝卡，妳今天下午要做什麼？）

W: I am going to Zhongshan Park with Alice.（女：我要和愛莉絲一起去中山公園。）

M: It's a better place to fly kites. You can also boat there.
（男：那是放風箏比較好的地方。妳也可以在那邊划船。）

W: But we are going there to have afternoon tea in a café. My friend Susan wants to discuss something with us.（女：但是我們要去那邊在一間咖啡廳喝下午茶。我的朋友蘇珊想要和我們討論一些事情。）

M: Enjoy your tea time.（男：好好享受妳們的午茶時間。）

Q: What is Rebecca going to do?（問題：瑞貝卡要做什麼？）

(A)To fly kites with Alice.（和愛莉絲一起放風箏。）
(B)To talk over something with friends.（和朋友們聊聊一些事情。）
(C)To go boating with her friends.（和朋友們一起划船。）
(D)To eat in a restaurant.（在一間餐廳裡吃飯。）

答案：(B)

12. M: I am so sorry to have kept you waiting for such a long time.
（男：我很抱歉讓您等了那麼長時間。）

W: That's all right. I was on the phone with my customer for twenty minutes and spent fifteen minutes reading today's newspaper. So time wasn't wasted.
（女：沒關係。我和我的客戶在電話上談了二十分中又花了十五分鐘看今天的報紙。所以時間沒有被浪費。）

M: How I wish I could have been here half an hour before. But you are really a kind person.（男：我多希望可以早半小時就在這裡。但是您真是個好人。）

Q: How long did the woman spend waiting for the man?
（問題：這位女士花了多少時間等這位男士？）

(A)30 min. (B)35 min. (C)20 min. (D)45 min.

答案：(B)

13. M: Do I have to take off the hat?（男：我需要脫帽嗎？）

W: Up to you. Are you ready?（女：隨便你。你準備好了嗎？）

M: OK. I hold it and then my face is clearly seen.
（男：好。我保持不動然後我的臉可以被看得很清楚。）

W: Yes, keep smiling.（女：對，保持微笑。）

Q: What are they doing now?（問題：他們現在正在做什麼？）
(A)Shopping for a hat.（採購一頂帽子。）
(B)Having the hair cut.（剪頭髮。）
(C)Dressing up.（穿戴整齊。）
(D)Taking a picture.（拍照。）
答案：(D)

14. M: I failed in my math test, Mom.（男：我數學考砸了，媽。）
    W: Poor guy. How did it happen? Did you have enough revision?
    （女：可憐的傢伙。這怎麼發生的？你有充分的複習嗎？）
    M: Yes. But I put the answers down in the wrong place.
    （男：有。但是我把答案寫在錯誤的地方了。）
    W: Don't worry. Have a good sleep and forget it.
    （女：別擔心。好好睡一覺忘了它吧。）
    Q: Why did the boy fail his math test?（問題：這位男孩為何數學考砸了？）
    (A)Because he was not careful enough.（因為他不夠小心。）
    (B)Because he didn't have a good sleep.（因為他睡得不好。）
    (C)Because he didn't have enough exercises.（因為他運動不足。）
    (D)Because he never put the notes down.（因為他沒有做筆記。）
    答案：(A)

15. M: Hello, may I speak to Mike?（男：哈囉，我可以和麥克講話嗎？）
    W: He isn't in. He will return in one and a half hours. Who is that speaking?
    （女：他不在耶。他會在一個半小時後回來。您哪裡找？）
    M: This is Jason, his classmate. I will call him at 5. Thank you.
    （男：我是傑森，他的同學。我五點會打電話給他。謝謝。）
    W: Not at all.（女：不謝。）
    Q: What time is it now?（問題：現在的時間是？）
    (A)Five o'clock.（五點整。）          (B)Half past two.（兩點半。）
    (C)Three thirty.（三點三十分。）       (D)Four thirty.（四點三十分。）
    答案：(C)

16. M: What happened to you, Alice?（男：妳怎麼了，愛莉絲？）
    W: A big fire destroyed my house and I don't know what to do with it.
    （女：一場大火毀了我的房子而我不知道該怎麼辦。）
    M: While we breathe, there is hope. Come on, Alice.
    （男：活著就有希望啊。振作點，愛莉絲。）
    Q: What can we learn from the man's words?
    （問題：從這位男士的話中我們可以得知？）
    (A)The man is the hope for Alice and he will help her.
    （這位男士是愛莉絲的希望，他會幫她。）
    (B)The man wants Alice to breathe deep to relax.

（這位男士希望愛莉絲深呼吸放輕鬆。）

(C)The man has pity on Alice, but he thinks everything will be better soon.

（這位男士同情愛莉絲，但他認為一切很快會變好。）

(D)The man wants Alice never to give up.（這位男士希望愛莉絲絕對不要放棄。）

答案：(D)

---

**Ⅲ Listen to the passage and tell whether the following statements are true or false.**
（判斷下列句子是否符合你聽到的短文內容,符合用 T 表示,不符合用 F 表示）（7分）

A Jefferson County teacher picked the wrong example when he used killing President Barack Obama as a way to teach math to his geometry students.

一位傑佛遜縣的老師選了個錯誤的例子,以殺害歐巴馬總統當做教幾何課學生的方法。

Someone told the police and the Corner High School math teacher was questioned by the police, but was not taken into prison or charged with any crime.

有個人去告訴警察而這位街角高中的老師就被警方偵訊,但沒有被抓去監獄或判任何罪。

The teacher was clearly teaching his geometry students about lines and angles. He used the example of where to stand and aim if shooting Obama with guns.

這位老師很明顯是在教他的幾何學生關於線和角度。他運用站在哪裡用槍射歐巴馬當做例子。

"He was talking about angles and said, 'If you're in this building, you would need to take this position to shoot the president,'" said a student in the geometry class.

「他是在講角度並且說,『如果你在建築物內,你會需要以這個定點來射擊總統,』」一位幾何班上的學生說。

"We are going to have a long conversation with him about what's proper," said the teacher who is in charge of the school. "It was extremely poor judgment on his part, and a poor choice of words."

「我們將要和他長談關於什麼是適當的,」掌管學校的這位老師說。「這是他這方面極為糟糕的判斷,並且是很糟糕的用詞。」

---

17. A teacher planned to kill President Obama.（一位老師計畫殺害歐巴馬總統。）

答案：(F 錯)

18. The mistake came from one of a math teacher's lessons.

（這錯誤來自一位數學老師的課堂。）

答案：(T 對)

19. The teacher was arrested and put into prison. （這位老師被逮捕並送入監獄。）
    答案：(F 錯)

20. In the lesson, the teacher talked about when and where to stand and aim if shooting Obama with the students.
    （在課堂上，這位老師對學生們講了關於如果要射擊歐巴馬，何時和站在何地瞄準。）
    答案：(F 錯)

21. The students found out the best position in a building to shoot Obama.
    （學生們發現了在建築物內射擊歐巴馬的最佳定點。）
    答案：(F 錯)

22. The school has decided to have a long talk with the teacher.
    （校方決定要跟這位老師長談。）
    答案：(T 對)

23. The school thinks that there is something wrong with the teacher's expressions.
    （校方認為這位老師的表達有些毛病。）
    答案：(T 對)

---

**IV. Listen to the poem and fill in the blanks with proper words.**（聽短詩,用最恰當的詞填空,每格限填一詞）（共 7 分）

---

Beloved country
我熱愛的國家
Ah! Of the motherland, you are the blue sky,
啊！祖國，你是藍天，
I was floating in the blue sky on a white cloud;
我在一朵藍天中的白雲上飄浮著；
Ah! Of the motherland, you are the sea,
啊！祖國，你是大海，
I am just the white sea spray;
我只是白色的浪花；
Ah! Of the motherland, you are the mountains,
啊！祖國，你是山，
I am a tall and straight tree on the mountain;
我是山上一棵又高又直的樹；
Ah! Of the motherland, you are a road leading to the distant, ah,
啊！祖國，你是一條通往遠處的路啊，
I was walking on this road one of the students to pursue a dream.
我是走在這條路上追夢的學生之一。

---

On your 60-year-old birthday,

在你六十歲的生日,

I want you to sing the Ode 60,

我想要你唱六十之頌,

I wish you will forever prosper;

我希望你永遠昌隆;

I want you to light 60 candles,

我要為你點燃六十根蠟燭,

Illuminates every corner of yours;

照亮你的每個角落;

I would also like for you to fly 60 doves of peace,

我也會想要為你放飛六十隻和平之鴿,

I wish you lasting peace and happiness...

我祝福你長久的和平與快樂...

- "Beloved country" is the title of a __24__.
  (「我熱愛的國家」是一首詩的題目。)
- Ah! Of the motherland, you are the blue sky, I was __25__ in the blue sky on a white cloud;
  (啊!你是祖國的藍天,我在一朵藍天中的白雲上飄浮著;)
- Ah! Of the motherland, you are the sea, I am just the __26__ sea spray;
  (啊!你是祖國的海,我只是白色的浪花;)
- Ah! Of the motherland, you are the mountains, I am a tall and __27__ tree on the mountain;
  (啊!你是祖國的山,我是山上一棵又高又直的樹;)
- Ah! Of the motherland, you are a road __28__ to the distant, ah, I was walking on this road one of the students to pursue a dream.
  (啊!你是祖國一條通往遠處的路,啊,我是走在這條路上追夢的學生之一。)
- On your 60-year-old birthday, I want you to sing the Ode 60. I wish you will __29__ prosper.
  (在你六十歲的生日,我想要你唱六十之頌,我希望你永遠昌隆。)
- I want you to light 60 candles, Illuminates every corner of yours; I would also like for you to fly 60 doves of peace, I wish you __30__ peace and happiness ...
  (我想要你點燃六十根蠟燭,照亮你的每個角落;我也會想要你讓六十隻和平鴿飛翔,我祝福你長久的和平與快樂...)

24. 答案:poem（詩）

25. 答案：floating（飄浮）
26. 答案：white（白色）
27. 答案：straight（直的）
28. 答案：leading（通往）
29. 答案：forever（永遠）
30. 答案：lasting（長久的）

# 筆記欄

# 筆 記 欄

# 筆記欄

夏朵英文